FROM division i... IN F... Y

By

Madison Robinson

A JESUS MAN

People Serving People
900 S. Arlington Avenue Suite 105B
Harrisburg, Pa. 17109
www.peopleservingpeopleharrisburg.com

Published by People Serving People Ministries
900 S Arlington Ave Ste 105B
Harrisburg, PA 17109

Ebook edition created 2015

ISBN 978-0-692-48833-1

Some names and details may have been changed to protect privacy.

FROM division in King James TO UNITY IN KING JESUS

Dedication Prayer:

TO THE ALL-KNOWING, LOVING, LIVING GOD AND FATHER OF US ALL. May all who read this book be filled with the knowledge of WHO YOU ARE? The world was made BY YOU, but knew YOU not. But we KNOW YOU, FOR YOU LIVE WITHIN US. FOR YOU ARE THE LIVING WORD OF GOD. FATHER, GLORIFY YOUR NAME. Amen.

To my loving wife whom I love with THE LOVE OF THE LORD. GOD HAS TRULY BLESSED me with you. FOR HE ENCOURAGED YOU to help me bring forth the song "GLORIFY YOUR NAME" and this book. I say thank you from the bottom of my Heart.

Introduction:

Every time HE IS mentioned, we must think of WHO HE IS. HIS NAME IS ALSO   HONORED AND POINTS TO WHO HE IS.

The purpose of this book is for us to KNOW AND EXPERIENCE THE SAME GOD they talked about in the Bible over thousands of years ago. Even today, GOD IS MANIFESTING HIMSELF to us in our trying times. We did not write this book to debate scripture. If I were to name a few of the other purposes for this book, they would be:

1. OUR GOD, FATHER AND CREATOR wants a closer relationship with us
     HIS created beings.

2. The next generation will need to KNOW THE TRUTH, for THE TRUTH
     HIMSELF will make them FREE.

3. To turn the Hearts of people to THE GOD the original writers
     ENCOUNTERED and EXPERIENCED.

This book is the fruit received from the offering of the song I gave to GOD, "GLORIFY YOUR NAME". One listener said that for him it was not just another worship song, but a worship experience. I am humbled by this response. To GOD BE THE GLORY. I trust that THE SPIRIT THAT INSPIRED me to write this book is THE SAME SPIRIT THAT WILL BLESS you to KNOW HIS VOICE and to not follow another.

Have you ever thought about what it means to have CHRIST IN YOU? IN HIS PRESENCE you come to KNOW HIS VOICE and to be led from the natural to THE SPIRITUAL REALM. HE WILL GUIDE you into HIS TRUTH. Experiencing the freedom that comes from HIS VOICE, BY GOD'S WORD is like being set free from prison after a lifetime behind bars. The more you give HIM your life, the more HE GIVES you HIS.

My earnest prayer is that whosoever reads this book will do so by THE LEADING OF THE SPIRIT OF GOD. Read it IN HIS PRESENCE. You are called to follow HIS

LEADING on an ongoing basis; therefore, you must make that decision on your own. OUR FATHER will not confuse us. HE would not have you to be double minded. Is there one Church or are there more? Who is "THE" Pastor? Is there another Word of God to live by other than HIMSELF?

By the time you finish reading this book you will understand what it's like to translate HIS LOVE, JOY, AND PEACE FROM THE KINGDOM within you. As you become ONE WITH GOD THROUGH HIS POWERFUL ALMIGHTY WORD and take on THE MIND OF CHRIST, HIS THOUGHTS will GOVERN everything you do. Staying IN HIS PRESENCE and worshiping HIM will make you a true worshipper. However, as long as you are governed by things that can be seen, then you are not submitted to THE SPIRIT THAT GIVES ETERNAL LIFE, PEACE, and UNITY. LIFE is far more than what can be seen.

In order for us to be one, as the answer to JESUS' prayer, we must make UNITY IN HIM our top priority. Then and only then can we be true representatives of THE KINGDOM OF GOD that is being restored to earth by JESUS. Right now, the fulfillment is coming through submitted sons who KNOW HIS VOICE and are teachable instead of self-centered children.
It seems like everybody that can't have their own way would like to start their own church. We've unknowingly taught our children to reject church by not teaching them that they are the church and together we are THE BODY OF CHRIST. HE is building people. Men build buildings.

Has THE FATHER REVEALED to you WHO JESUS IS, like HE DID to Peter? Let's seek HIM together. Every time we come together, the location can be called a house of prayer for "all people" where THE CHURCH congregates.

Chapter One

GOD'S WORD, Man's Words

We must look past that which is called obvious, past the things that make good sense to the natural mind, and past the thoughts and opinions of self-exalted religious professionals and the organizations they lead. Everyone seems to be drawn to their own group and their own opinions. But, out of every nation the LORD IS CALLING FORTH HIS TRUE CHURCH. Who will HEAR HIM and respond? It is THE LORD WHO WILL PREVAIL.

For those who have read the scriptures, you may want to read your bible again while acknowledging THE WORD OF GOD IN THE PERSON OF JESUS. For those of you who have not read the Bible yet, you are challenged to read one for yourself. Learn to always look unto THE SPIRIT OF TRUTH TO SPEAK IN BETWEEN every word and line in the book. You will have to search the scriptures for yourselves. No matter which version, you will still have to LEARN TO HEAR WHAT THE SPIRIT IS SAYING to you personally.

If you go into this book with the idea that it is somehow an assault on your Bible, which is not my intention. Don't be deceived about this. Use every tool you can. Read every bible version you like, and listen to every preacher prayerfully, but know this: THE ALMIGHTY WORD OF GOD IS GOD!

Some may accuse me of attacking the so-called inerrancy of Scripture. (Inerrant is just a theological word that means, "Without error").

If this means the Bible has no mistakes then let me ask you this question: Which Translations of the Bible are we talking about out of thousands? Which one is inerrant?

What THE SPIRIT IS SAYING (in my own words) is: "if you make your preferred versions and interpretations EQUAL TO HIM, you have been deceived in the worst way. "In the beginning was the Word . . .". Don't settle for anything less than the Truth, the Spirit, and THE VOICE OF HIM WHO STANDS ALONE, THE ALMIGHTY WORD OUR CREATOR. HE WHO SPEAKS FOR HIMSELF, AND GIVES LIFE TO WHAT HE SAYS AND REVEALS WHAT HE MEANS, HE WANTS TO LIVE WITHIN US".

When GOD'S WORD COMES TO CORRECT, you don't want to be like the religious leaders who made the letter say what they wanted it to say. This adds to the confusion and division orchestrated by the father of lies. JESUS SAID (and it was recorded in Scripture) that If you don't HEAR HIS VOICE you are none of HIS. Can You HEAR HIM TO BELIEVE?

1 I, therefore, the prisoner of THE LORD, beseech you to walk worthy of the calling with which you were called, 2 with all lowliness and gentleness, with longsuffering, bearing with one another in
Love, 3 endeavoring to keep THE UNITY OF THE SPIRIT in the bond of PEACE. 4 There is ONE BODY and ONE SPIRIT, just as you were called in ONE HOPE of your calling; 5 ONE LORD, ONE FAITH, ONE BAPTISM; 6 ONE GOD

AND FATHER of all, WHO IS ABOVE all, and through all, and in you all. 7 But to each one of Us GRACE was given according to the measure of CHRIST'S GIFT. (Ephesians 4:1-7 NKJV)

Again, you who have read the Bible "MUST" read it again while acknowledging THE WORD OF GOD FOR WHO HE IS. JESUS' NAME IS THE BRIDGE BACK TO WHO HE IS, OUR FATHER'S WORD MADE FLESH. For those of you who have not read the Bible yet, you can purchase one at the dollar store if you can't afford to buy one anywhere else. But again, you also "MUST" have an ear to HEAR HIM WHO CAN MAKE HIMSELF KNOWN LIKE none other AND WRITE THE EXPERIENCE OF KNOWING WHAT HE SAID AND MEANT ON YOUR HEART. HIS SPIRIT WILL ALWAYS BE NEAR TO LEAD, GUIDE, PROTECT, AND CORRECT as long as your free will is subject TO HIS WORD OF CORRECTION AS SONS. Read Hebrews 12:5-11. In learning to KNOW THE VOICE AND THE WORD OF OUR FATHER, we will purpose to make everything we read Line up WITH WHAT HIS SPIRIT SAYS, FIRST HAND.

HE WHO SPOKE TO the first Adam in the garden SPEAKS TO us who have access INTO HIS GLORIOUS KINGDOM OF LOVE, JOY, AND PEACE IN THE HOLY GHOST.
And he or she who has BEEN GIVEN A SPIRITUAL EAR MADE TO HEAR HIS VOICE THAT CAN CAUSE Mountains to quake OR SPEAK PEACE TO The winds AND TELL THE waves to BE STILL. HE SPOKE ALSO

11

OF VICTORY OVER ALL THE SUFFERING AND SHAME HE HAD TO ENDURE FOR US. BEFORE HE BECAME A MAN HE SPOKE OF HIS DEATH, BURIAL, AND RESURRECTION. HIS HOLY SPIRIT IS HIS OWN GREATEST   WITNESS TO male and female alike. I PRAY that as you read or whenever you turn your ear and eyes toward HIM TO TRULY KNOW HIM BY HIS WORD that you know that there are many fallen spirits that lie and will try and distract, confuse and disrupt you from spending the time necessary TO KNOW HIM BY HIS OWN WORD DIRECTLY TO YOU. Delivering you from people who are deceived in thinking man's knowledge of another version of God's word, that some have claimed to have mastered, is the equivalent of THE CREATOR OF THE WHOLE universe MAKING HIMSELF KNOWN TO those who have come to an end of themselves. Unashamed to admit unto our LIFE SOURCE that all the knowledge we have learned outside THE KINGDOM OF TRUTH AND RIGHTOUSNESS is still limited to good and evil. But, just in case there are still some that believe holding on to their position in man's governmental order is more important than to submit to THE LIVING WORD, think about this: There are about 400 different versions of the Bible and countless different personal interpretations. How can all of these possibly be the only infallible Word of God?

Most confessing Christians are content to be a part of their own separate church group. After all, everyone's doing it. We've been like little children who want to have their own way and that everyone has their own church where they keep to themselves.

When we REALLY COME TO HEAR THE WORD OF
GOD, how can we not come together IN HIS LOVE,
LONGSUFFERING, FORGIVENESS, WISDOM,
PEACE AND POWER?

Together, let us expose the works of the deceiver and
openly PREACH JESUS   with the full assurance of
HEAVEN BACKING HIS WORD, through us! You are
challenged to read or re-read your bible "AND" seek THE
SPIRIT OF TRUTH.

Remember that a spirit of unbelief will always be able to
find a scripture to support its unbelief and unwillingness to
obey GOD'S WORD.   I believe that as we grow up and
put away our "childish things," we will move IN THE
SPIRIT OF JESUS' PRAYER FOR US TO BE ONE!

Let's look at JESUS' PRAYER for us in John 17 but, first,
let's talk about money. THE SPIRIT OF WISDOM that
INSTRUCTED Solomon ALSO GAVE him wealth. THE
SPIRIT OF WISDOM lets us KNOW THAT we too must
have a heart for the people.   He instructs us not to chase
after money for WISDOM TELLS US that the earth was
given to us. BLESSED are the meek for they shall inherit
the earth. No amount of money compares to that which
was restored back to us by JESUS' FINISHED WORK.

OBEY THE WORD HE GIVES you and watch the money
chase after you. GOD always will provide for HIS
DESIRE. There are things we must learn from THE
SPIRIT OF WISDOM to prepare us to handle the wealth
HE would gladly, supernaturally give us. But what would
happen if the BLESSINGS HE WANTS to put in our
hands came regardless of our behavior? We would end up

as unprofitable stewards and it would probably end up in the hands of unjust people. This is not GOD'S DESIRE.

I want you to do yourself a big favor and re-read how JESUS MET the needs of everyone who asked in FAITH. Notice how easy it was. All HE HAD TO DO WAS SAY A WORD! Do you HEAR WHAT THE SPIRIT IS SAYING RIGHT NOW? BELIEVE even if your faith is tried. Even if the answer is sometimes delayed, BELIEVE. HIS SPIRIT OF WISDOM IS CALLING us from division in King James to unity in King JESUS. He is calling us from men's words TO HIS Word. So, using your preferred translation of scripture, let's look at what THE WORD OF GOD IN THE FLESH SAID as recorded by John in Chapter 17:1-26 (NKJV):

1 Jesus spoke these words, lifted up his eyes to heaven, and said: FATHER, THE HOUR HAS COME. GLORIFY YOUR SON, THAT YOUR SON ALSO MAY GLORIFY YOU, 2 as you have given Him authority over all flesh, that He should give eternal life to as many as you have given Him. 3 And this is eternal life that they may know you, the only true God, and Jesus Christ whom you have sent. 4 I have glorified You on the earth. I have finished the work which You have given Me to do. 5 And now, O Father, glorify Me together with Yourself, with the glory which I had with You before the world was.

Jesus Prays for His Disciples

6 "I have manifested Your name to the men whom You have given Me out of the world. They were Yours, You gave them to Me, and they have kept Your word. 7 Now

they have known that all things which You have given Me are from You. ⁸ For I have given to them the words which You have given Me; and they have received *them,* and have known surely that I came forth from You; and they have believed that You sent Me.

⁹ "I pray for them. I do not pray for the world but for those whom You have given Me, for they are Yours. ¹⁰ And all Mine are Yours, and Yours are Mine, and I am glorified in them. ¹¹ Now I am no longer in the world, but these are in the world, and I come to You. Holy Father, keep through Your name those whom You have given Me, that they may be one as We *are.* ¹² While I was with them in the world, I kept them in Your name. Those whom You gave Me I have kept; and none of them is lost except the son of perdition, that the Scripture might be fulfilled. ¹³ But now I come to You, and these things I speak in the world, that they may have My joy fulfilled in themselves. ¹⁴ I have given them Your word; and the world has hated them because they are not of the world, just as I am not of the world. ¹⁵ I do not pray that You should take them out of the world, but that You should keep them from the evil one. ¹⁶ They are not of the world, just as I am not of the world. ¹⁷ Sanctify them by Your truth. Your word is truth. ¹⁸ As You sent Me into the world, I also have sent them into the world. ¹⁹ And for their sakes I sanctify Myself, that they also may be sanctified by the truth.

Jesus Prays for All Believers

²⁰ "I do not pray for these alone, but also for those who will believe in Me through their word; ²¹ that they all may be

one, as You, Father, *are* in Me, and I in You; that they also may be one in Us, that the world may believe that You sent Me. [22] And the glory which You gave Me I have given them, that they may be one just as We are one: [23] I in them, and You in Me; that they may be made perfect in one, and that the world may know that You have sent Me, and have loved them as You have loved Me.

[24] "Father, I desire that they also whom You gave Me may be with Me where I am, that they may behold My glory which You have given Me; for You loved Me before the foundation of the world. [25] O righteous Father! The world has not known You, but I have known You; and these have known that You sent Me. [26] And I have declared to them Your name, and will declare *it,* that the love with which You loved Me may be in them, and I in them."

If you find yourself in the bondage of traditions and doctrines of men, my question to you would be: is GOD the author of confusion, misunderstanding, misinterpretation and ungodly divisions?

Look again at the root of it all. Anyone not MADE ONE IN GOD'S WORD could be on the wrong road headed in the wrong direction. Scripture interpreted correctly shows us JESUS IS THE WAY THE TRUTH AND THE LIFE. Bondage is the result of deception in choosing another word that is not GOD'S. In other Words, not hearing, not knowing, and not following the voice of JESUS. HE is the fulfillment of all Truth and doesn't exclude anyone from being all that they were created to be. Everyone who finds their place IN HIM, finds COMPLETE SATISFACTION in HIM. BLESSED are those humble enough to receive HIS WISDOM THAT GIVES them power IN "His Word!" (GOD'S LIVING WORD IS THE TRUTH.) Here are a few things that are opposed to THE SPIRIT OF TRUTH:

1 . A lack of knowledge of (HIS TRUTH);
2 . Failure to submit to HIS TRUTH;
3 . Idolatry of the Bible (It doesn't matter which version. Idolatry is sin), and
4 . Not recognizing the difference between the under shepherd and   THE SHEPHERD.

Now, here is what separates the children from the mature SONS OF GOD -- The children are still self-centered, seeking their own way. Everything is about me, my, and I. JESUS REVEALED the focus of the Son TO THE FATHER in Matthew 6:8-13 (NKJV)

[8] "Therefore do not be like them. For your Father knows the things you have need of before you ask Him. [9] In this manner, therefore, pray:

Our Father in heaven, Hallowed be Your name. [10] Your kingdom come.
Your will be done On earth as *it is* in heaven. [11] Give us this day our daily bread. [12] And forgive us our debts, As we forgive our debtors.
[13] And do not lead us into temptation, But deliver us from the evil one.
For Yours is the kingdom and the power and the glory forever. Amen.

Tradition has taught us to say the bible is the Word of God. My question is: which translation is the Word? There's a major problem in just calling the Bible in and of itself the Word of God. Did it, the Bible, create all things? THE WORD OF GOD IS GOD, WHO GIVES LIFE, AND UNDERSTANDING unto the simple. When HE SPEAKS, all creation must obey HIS VOICE. HEALING COMES FROM HIM, DELIVERANCE, WISDOM, KNOWLEDGE, AND THE POWER to get wealth. Nothing I can think of can compare to the WORD OF GOD. Does that describe the Bible?

We are called to receive JESUS and in Him we find all THE FULFILLMENT of THE ORIGINAL TRUTH GIVEN. Every jot and tittle:

Matthew 5:18 (KJV): "For verily I say unto you, Till heaven and earth pass, one jot or one tittle shall in no wise pass from the law, till all be fulfilled" (A tittle is just the dot over a lower case i or j)

THE Bible contains some direct quotes from GOD, even those of THE WORD MADE FLESH. But there are direct quotes of men, both good and evil ones in there, too. Spirits that oppose THE TRUTH have a Word or two in there. Are these translations THE WORD OF GOD that HE HONORS ABOVE HIS NAME? Think about it!

Where is THE POWER TO LOVE and submit to one another? Why have we not become one through reading and studying the Bible? We disagree constantly about what things mean in it. Deceitful men are able to make it say just about anything they want depending on what they're trying to accomplish.

You and I must understand the purpose of the Bible. GOD never intended for it to take the place of THE WORD OF GOD WHO SPEAKS. It, the Bible, is not a short cut to THE FATHER. We each must have our own relationship with HIM WHO KNOWS the hearts of every man. WHAT HE, THE LIVING WORD SAID over two thousand years ago still applies. "No man cometh unto the Father but by me". Our Bibles are only a means to HIM. HE was here before King James and every other translation that points us to THE TRUE AND LIVING GOD. That's their purpose I pray. Think please before you call any Bible THE WORD OF GOD again. The Bible is a book. Even though you're trying to get people to believe on JESUS, preach and teach THE WORD OF GOD and point people to HIM. Bible or no bible, PREACH JESUS! HE IS THE ETERNAL, LIVING WORD OF ALMIGHTY GOD.

1 Timothy 3:16 (NKJV)

16 And without controversy great is the mystery of godliness: God was manifested in the flesh, Justified in the Spirit, Seen by angels, Preached among the Gentiles, Believed on in the world, Received up in glory.

Chapter Two

THE FATHER GLORIFIES THE SON

John 1:1-14 (KJV)

"1 In the beginning was the Word, and the Word was with God, and the Word was God. 2 The same was in the beginning with God. 3 All things were made by him; and without him was not any thing made that was made. 4 In him was life; and the life was the light of men. 5 And the light shineth in darkness; and the darkness comprehended it not. 6 There was a man sent from God, whose name was John. 7 The same came for a witness, to bear witness of the Light, that all men through him might believe. 8 He was not that Light, but was sent to bear witness of that Light. 9 That was the true Light, which lighteth every man that cometh into the world. 10 He was in the world, and the world was made by him, and the world knew him not 11 He came unto his own, and his own received him not. 12 But as many as received him, to them gave he power to become the sons of God, even to them that believe on his name: 13 Which were born, not of blood, nor of the will of the flesh, nor of the will of man, but of God. 14 And the Word was made flesh, and dwelt among us, (and we beheld his glory, the glory as of the only begotten of the Father,) full of grace and truth."

THE KINGDOM OF GOD has been RESTORED back to man by the FINISHED WORK OF JESUS. Here's a key to unlocking the mystery: HE IS THE ONLY TRUE AND LIVING WORD OF GOD. Your challenge is to seek THE WORD OF GOD and to ALLOW HIS SPIRIT to make

scripture line up with HIM. Remember! THE FATHER
GLORIFIES THE SON. JESUS IS THE SON.

John explained it this way: "In the beginning was THE
WORD and THE WORD WAS WITH GOD." We should
always thank GOD for the finished work of HIS WORD
MADE FLESH. HIS WORD WAS GIVEN THE NAME
JESUS. We must be perfectly clear about Who THE SON
IS and HIS RELATIONSHIP TO HIS FATHER.
Now as we read about JESUS, we must receive "THE
SPIRIT OF WHO HE TRULY IS." Seeing JESUS, THE
WORD OF GOD leads us to not just read the Bible like
reading the daily news, but we seek to hear from THE
ONE WHO STILL SPEAKS AND GIVES TRUE
UNDERSTANDING. Reading while being LED BY THE
SPIRIT, changes the very way you read. It is like the
WORD FROM GOD is standing out in bold capital letters.

We should always be mindful of HIS KINGDOM restored
back to us by THE LAST ADAM. We should always be
aware of HIS KINGDOM WITHIN US and carry
ourselves as REPRESENTATIVES OF THAT ETERNAL
KINGDOM where everything IN IT is subject to THE
WORD OF THE KING. Now we see THE WORD OF
GOD CALLED JESUS WALKING ON EARTH to show
plainly THE WAY OF TRUTH. For HE SAID WITH HIS
WORDS, HE WAS THE WAY, THE TRUTH AND THE
LIFE. No man cometh unto the Father but by Me (John
14:6).

Whenever you confess JESUS AS THE TRUE AND
LIVING WORD OF GOD don't be surprised at the
response you get. People are so programmed to live by,

and be governed by, what they see with their natural eyes. When preaching JESUS, THE WORD, some people will justify themselves and one of the first things people will say without thinking to inquire of God is: "well the Bible is the Word of God too." There is no sound scripture support for any Bible being THE WORD OF GOD. Which one? There are numerous Bible versions. Then instead of repenting they try and make sense out of what they said with some of the most ridiculous statements you will ever hear. And, the more they try and justify what they mean, the more outrageous they sound.

I can't understand how King James or any other version of the Bible became THE WORD OF GOD. How did people come to confuse our written Words with THE LIVING GOD? We repeat these kinds of statements because there are years of tradition that go deep, real deep into the hearts of many people.

So far, we have established beyond any shadow of doubt that THE LIVING WORD OF GOD IS GOD. Before the world began, HE WAS GOD. All things were CREATED BY GOD'S EXISTENCE BY HIS WORD. Now, let's take some time to look at JESUS, THE WORD MADE FLESH. HE WAS GIVEN A NAME above every name, "That at THE NAME OF JESUS every knee should bow of things IN HEAVEN and things in earth and things under the earth." And that every tongue should confess that JESUS CHRIST IS LORD TO THE GLORY OF GOD THE FATHER" (Phil 2:10, 11). If HIS NAME IS THAT POWERFUL, how much more powerful would it be if we KNOW HIM TO WHOM THE NAME WAS GIVEN? In fact, the only thing HE PLACED ABOVE HIS

23

NAME WAS "HIS WORD, "not man's understanding or the best Christian bible school in the world, only HIS WORD. For who can instruct HIM? The good news is – "HE CAME UNTO HIS OWN and HIS OWN received HIM NOT. But as many as RECEIVED HIM, TO THEM HE GAVE POWER TO BECOME THE SONS OF GOD, even to them that believe on HIS NAME" (John 1:11-12).

Is the WORD OF GOD SPIRIT AND TRUTH or pen and paper? Are all the religious Bibles the Word of God? Or, just the King James Version? Do you have a certain version you prefer? Which one is it? And, what makes that version the only infallible inspired version that you would build your eternal foundation upon?

I hope you love reading scripture, especially after knowing that THE SAME WORD OF GOD WHO SPOKE to people from the beginning of time IS STILL SPEAKING TO "anyone that has an ear to hear what HIS SPIRIT IS SAYING". Here is a passage from Luke:

Luke 4:17-21(NKJV)

17 And He was handed the book of the prophet Isaiah. And when He had opened the book, He found the place where it was written: 18 "The Spirit of the Lord is upon Me, Because He has anointed Me To preach the gospel to the poor; He has sent Me to heal the brokenhearted, To proclaim liberty to the captives And recovery of sight to the blind, To set at liberty those who are oppressed; 19 To proclaim the acceptable year of the Lord." 20 Then He closed the book, and gave it back to the attendant and sat

down. And the eyes of all who were in the synagogue were fixed on Him. 21 And He began to say to them, "Today this Scripture is fulfilled in your hearing."

KNOWING HIM and looking at everything JESUS SAID AND DID, we understand that HIS WILL AND PURPOSE HAD TO COME TO PASS, FOR HE WAS AND IS THE WORD OF GOD THAT CANNOT LIE. We should obey and trust HIS WORD just like Simon Peter did when JESUS, THE WORD OF GOD, told Him to launch out into the deep and let down his nets for a great load of fish. Even though they had been toiling all night and unable to catch anything, they obeyed (read Luke 5:4-11).

THE WORDS OF JESUS are unlike any other man's Words. HE SPEAKS AND IT IS DONE; FOR THE FATHER GLORIFIES THE SON. Let's look at Luke's account of the POWER IN GOD'S WORD TO HEAL ALL. Read Luke 6:17-19, 27, 28 followed by Luke 6:47-49.

Now read Luke 7:1-10. If you have truly understood all you've read this far, you will never look at these scriptures the same way again. Your ears will be tuned into hearing A WORD directly and tailor made, just for you. I pray you have the humility to let THE LIVING WORD MANIFEST IN AND THROUGH YOU.

One more message out of Luke I want to leave with you is found in the 8th Chapter of Luke where we read THE WORD OF GOD MADE FLESH sharing the parable of

the sower (read Luke 8:9-15). Re-read these verses until
the Truth is understood in your innermost being, especially
verses 10 and 15. We're still dealing with the relationship
between JESUS, THE WORD OF GOD AND THE
FATHER. THE SON ALWAYS HONORED THE
FATHER, AND THE FATHER, THE SON.

I remember when I first started to HEAR and understand
that what I was HEARING was indeed THE WORD OF
GOD. The things I heard were too wonderful to be my
words or anyone else's. And even when reading, HE
SHOWED me that after HEARING AND KNOWING HIS
WORD the mere words of men don't impress anywhere
near as much. Now, in HEARING HIM, HE HAS GIVEN
what was missing when I first started reading: LIFE TO
MY UNDERSTANDING. FOR HE IS THE LIVING
FUFILLMENT OF what we read, FOR EVERYONE IN
UNITY WITH HIM WANTS THE SAME THING -- FOR
HIM TO BE KNOWN.

Matthew 6:33 (NKJV)

33 "But seek first the kingdom of God and His
righteousness, and all these things shall be added to you."

My wife and I are ministers of finance. We teach people
certain truths about wealth. For example: THE WORD OF
GOD SPOKE to Solomon, and Solomon had to receive
instructions from THE SPIRIT OF WISDOM and adhere
to what he heard. Solomon became wise because of THE

POWER IN THE WORD OF GOD to accomplish just
what THE ALMIGHTY WORD IN HIM PURPOSED.

Proverbs 10:22 (KJV) says, "The blessing of the LORD, it
maketh rich, and HE addeth no sorrow with it."

THE SAME SPIRIT OF WISDOM that Solomon received
is still in operation in THE PURPOSE OF GOD for those
who can hear Him. We'll go into more detail about wealth
in another book, but our goal for you in this one is to first
make sure you understand that the key TO THE
KINGDOM IS IN KNOWING WHO JESUS IS like Peter
in Mark 8:27. (INSPIRED BY THE SPIRIT, I was given a
song called "WHO DO YOU SAY I AM" but that story is
for another time).

Chapter Three

GLORIFY YOUR NAME IN US or THE FATHER GLORIFIES HIS NAME IN US

I remember it as though it was yesterday. I was walking around in the sanctuary of a local assembly praying and thanking GOD FOR ALL HE HAS DONE and seeking HIM FOR A WORD OF DIRECTION. I remember running out of Words to say. Then, up out of my spirit came: "GLORIFY YOUR NAME, GLORIFY YOUR NAME, GLORIFY YOUR NAME TODAY IN YOUR OWN WAY, GLORIFY YOUR NAME TODAY, FATHER, GLORIFY YOUR NAME, GLORIFY YOUR NAME, GLORIFY YOUR NAME TODAY, IN YOUR OWN WAY, GLORIFY YOUR NAME TODAY. That's why I'm calling JESUS, JESUS GLORIFY YOUR NAME TODAY, HOLY SPIRIT, HOLY SPIRIT, HOLY SPIRIT, MOVE TODAY, IN YOUR OWN WAY, HOLY SPIRIT MOVE...TODAY."

That was my own personal offering unto God, I considered it PRICELESS! From time to time, people would hear it, and just like my number one encourager, friend and "help meet" Diona, my wife for over 50 years, they too tried to encourage me to record it. I was convinced no one was going to make me reduce my PRICELESS OFFERING UNTO GOD down to a dollar amount. IN HEAVEN PRICELESS means PRICELESS. But, here on earth we're subject to changing our minds as we "learn" to say what THE SPIRIT OF TRUTH SAYS. Because HE GAVE IT TO GIVE TO THE WORLD, ALL THAT IS ETERNAL IN HIM IS PRICELESS.

Well, after years of having a made up mind, resisting what I considered a nagging wife who didn't understand, I came to see that my wife HEARS FROM GOD TOO. When a mutual friend of ours referred us to a friend of theirs who lived in Connecticut who had a recording studio in his home, I agreed to talk to him by phone. His name was Dennis Grady. After talking with Dennis for about 15 to 20 minutes, our spirits agreed because he had such a humble spirit and that conversation changed my mind about recording it, but I still didn't like the idea of reducing my PRICELESS gift down to $8.95. Well the cd can be sold but THE SPIRIT IS FREE. Music is also a tool like our bibles that should point us TO HIM WHO SPEAKS FOR HIMSELF.

Not long after that phone call, I went to GOD to give me the words to finish the Song. To my amazement, the words seemed to just flow from HEAVEN nonstop. I sent the words and melody to Dennis and, in no time at all, he sent me the music tape, straight from HEAVEN. Now I'm excited! My wife and encourager made the arrangements for me to go to Connecticut. I fasted and in about four hours, I was done. When I woke up the next morning, Dennis had added the background and completed the whole song. When I heard it, I could hardly believe what my ears heard. The first four verses were my perfect offering TO GOD as seed. The message from OUR FATHER to us is an answer to the prayers of everyone who want HIS WILL TO BE DONE ON EARTH WHICH BRINGS GLORY TO HIS NAME FOR MAKING OUR FATHER'S WILL KNOWN TO MAN, showing each other HIS LOVE is THE WAY. AND KNOWING WHO

JESUS IS, WE TURN OUR EARS TO HIM TO BE LED
BY HIM.

HE gave me these words to share with you. They are
found in 2 Chronicles 7:14 which you can read using your
preferred translations of scripture. If you haven't
memorized this verse, please don't forget THE TRUTH
OF ALL HE EVER SAID AND MEANT IS IN HIS
SPIRIT.

This song and book should be in every believer's
possession. As his PEOPLE, called by HIS NAME
together obey those verses "AS HIS PEOPLE" HE said,
not me or the translators but THE VERY MERCIFUL,
CREATIVE WORD WHO NEVER LIES, SAID HE
WOULD FORGIVE OUR SIN AND HEAL OUR LAND
FOR HE IS NOT a respecter of persons.

Looking back over the priceless piece of music that was
within me and was almost withheld from the rest of THE
BODY OF CHRIST, I must think of all the wonderful
things lying dormant within you. I hope for your sake that
GOD would use someone in your life to continue to
pressure you to SEEK HIM for what would turn out to be a
much more PERFECT OFFERING OF OBEDIENCE.
Find out THE GIFT GOD has given you and obediently
flow in it. You will be amazed how mighty THE LORD
will use you when you FLOW IN HIM AND HE IN YOU.
You're one of a kind. There's no one like you who can do
what you're called to do the way only you can do it.

Remember, the obedience of us all outweighs the perfect personal offering any one of us could make alone. Please understand that a body has different parts and each part is important, we can only be PERFECTED BY GOD, WHO gave all the gifts working together with the same agendas "for the perfecting of the saints for the work of the ministry for the edifying of THE BODY OF CHRIST." The world must see JESUS WHO we preach (Read Ephesians 4:12-16). In light of that, do you see how important your offering is? And why God gave it to you in the first place? For some of you, all you need to know is you're no longer your own -- that you have been BOUGHT WITH A PRICE. Yet, THE GREATEST SACRIFICE IS THE ONE GOD GAVE. HE GAVE THE ONLY TRUE PERFECT OFFERING IN THE PERSON OF JESUS, HIS WORD MADE FLESH. JESUS IS THE PERFECT OFFERING WHO GAVE HIS VERY LIFE. All we have to give is our wills so our gifts can be used TO THE GLORY OF GOD. ONLY GOD IN MAN, THE WORD MADE FLESH, COULD HAVE BEEN THAT PERFECT OFFERING for the sins of the whole world. Anything or anyone else would have collapsed under the weight of all that was placed on Him. Look at His ACTIONS IN THE GARDEN OF GETHSEMANE. FOR THE WORD OF GOD THROUGH JESUS SAID, "MY SOUL IS EXCEEDING SORROWFUL UNTO DEATH." Mark 14:34. Remember, it's not the translation that speaks but THE SPIRIT OF HIM WHO SAID, "LET US MAKE MAN".

Chapter Four

UNITY

THE LORD IS BUILDING HIS CHURCH AND
EVERYONE WHO CAN HEAR HIS VOICE will come
out of division into UNITY IN HIM. As I said in Chapter
One, "We must look past that which is called obvious, past
the things that make good sense to the natural mind, and
past the thoughts and opinions of religious professionals
and the organizations they lead. Everyone seems to be
drawn to their own group and their own opinions. But out
of every nation THE LORD IS CALLING FORTH HIS
TRUE CHURCH Who will HEAR HIM and respond in
such a way as to be CHOSEN?

This could very well be my favorite part of this book
because of the things GOD WILL DO when we receive
HIS SPIRIT OF UNITY. HE WILL make the world see
THE MESSAGE OF LOVE HE HAS BEEN TRYING TO
GET US TO SEE from the beginning. All of creation is
waiting for the manifestation of THE SONS OF GOD. If
you do not come into unity with THE SPIRIT OF TRUTH,
you will not fully understand what I've written thus far.
Until your Spirit is made ALIVE UNTO HIM, THE
TRUTH, you are limited to debating scripture. Can you
imagine how many times THE WORD OF GOD COMES
to people and they, out of tradition, challenge Him with
their interpretation of scriptures?
I hope the scriptures I've used have helped you to
understand their purpose, for the scriptures were never
meant to take the place of THE WORD OF GOD, but
point us to HIM. During the time when the original

writers began to write, not in English but in their own original languages, they were pointing people TO HIM, THE LIVING WORD.

Only after RECEIVING FAVOR BY THE WORD OF GOD, BY HIS WORD, ARE WE GIVEN ACCESS INTO HIS ETERNAL KINGDOM RESTORED BACK TO US RIGHT NOW! WHEREVER THE WORD OF GOD IS, BEHOLD THE KINGDOM IS AT HAND. IF THE WORD OF GOD WHO IS GOD HAS RULE IN YOUR HEART YOU WILL BE CONVERTED. NOT you BUT THE WORD DIRECTING YOU. So don't become like the one man band, or start your own church. Because far too many people who THE LORD HAVE USED today really think they are the star of the show and their name is up in lights and you have to look real hard to find JESUS' NAME anywhere. If you or this generation rejects THE SPIRIT OF UNITY IN JESUS, you also reject THE SPIRIT OF WISDOM WHO LEADS US OUT of deception, division, pride, idolatry, self-exaltation, and a deaf and dumb spirit. Unable to HEAR THE VOICE OF GOD OR TO KNOW HIS WORD OF TRUTH, how will you be led into ALL TRUTH? How bad do things have to get before people who know all the scriptures come to an end of themselves and stop looking at Capitol Hill as if they could heal the land? Let's change our tactics. Instead of pointing the finger at others, let's look in our own backyard and clean up the mess we have going on. If this generation refuses to turn unto THE WORD OF GOD, then they will continue to pride themselves in all the good works they're doing, pointing out all the evil in the world as if the world can help being the world. When they look at the traditional   bible-believing churchgoers, what do they see? Confusion, misunderstanding, division? If division was cast out of HEAVEN before the world began, know that division will not be tolerated in His Kingdom today! There is no division in HIM, AT ALL! No division in THE FATHER, THE SON OR THE HOLY GHOST. The reason we stress and repeat these things is because the roots of deception go all the way back to the garden. And as soon as some people put this book down, like the bible, they will go right back to business as usual.

I remember the day I thought in my mind that I was the most important thing in the world when I went into this little storefront house of prayer. I don't remember what the message was on that day, but I never will forget recognizing THE SPIRIT OF GOD that was on those few folk. Then I KNEW what my soul had been looking for, for over 30 years. And, I KNEW THIS WAS WHAT I WANTED. That very day I was a changed man. I didn't have THE Spirit to the extent they did, but I KNEW I was on the right road headed in the right direction in SEEKING HIM until I was found of HIM. And, today forty years later, I'm pleading with you to really seek to HEAR HIM TO BE CHANGED BY HIM if you are to be HIS. YOU MUST COME TO KNOW HIS VOICE.

There are only two churches mentioned in scripture. THE LORD's CHURCH in many different locations and the harlot church. HIS CHURCH WILL BE SUBJECT TO HIS WORD AND NOT DECEIVED BY ANOTHER.

Listen to Paul writing to the Ephesians in Ephesians Chapter 4:1-24 (NKJV):

1 "I, therefore, the prisoner of the Lord, beseech you to walk worthy of the calling with which you were called, 2 with all lowliness and gentleness, with longsuffering, bearing with one another in love, 3 endeavoring to keep the unity of the Spirit in the bond of peace. 4 There is one body and one Spirit, just as you were called in one hope of your calling; 5 one Lord, one faith, one baptism; 6 one God and Father of all, who is above all, and through all, and in you all. 7 But to each one of us grace was given according to the measure of Christ's gift. 8 Therefore He says:

"When He ascended on high, He led captivity captive, And gave gifts to men."[b]9 (Now this, "He ascended"—what does it mean but that He also first[c] descended into the lower parts of the earth? 10 He who descended is also the One who ascended far above all the heavens, that He might fill all things.) 11 And He Himself gave some to be apostles, some prophets, some evangelists, and some pastors and teachers, 12 for the equipping of the saints for the work of ministry, for the edifying of the body of Christ, 13 till we all come to the unity of the faith and of the knowledge of the Son of God, to a perfect man, to the measure of the stature of the fullness of Christ; 14 that we should no longer be children, tossed to and fro and carried about with every wind of doctrine, by the trickery of men, in the cunning craftiness of deceitful plotting, 15 but, speaking the truth in love, may grow up in all things into Him who is the head—Christ— 16 from whom the whole body, joined and knit together by what every joint supplies, according to the effective working by which every part does its share, causes growth of the body for the edifying of itself in love. 17 This I say, therefore, and testify in the Lord, that you should no longer walk as the rest of[d] the Gentiles walk, in the futility of their mind, 18 having their understanding darkened, being alienated from the life of God, because of the ignorance that is in them, because of the blindness of their heart; 19 who, being past feeling, have given themselves over to lewdness, to work all uncleanness with greediness. 20 But you have not so learned Christ, 21 if indeed you have heard Him and have been taught by Him, as the truth is in Jesus: 22 that you put off, concerning your former conduct, the old man which grows corrupt according to the deceitful lusts, 23 and be renewed in the spirit of your mind, 24 and that you put on the new man which was created according to God, in true righteousness and holiness."

Where is all THE RIGHTOUSNESS AND HOLINESS ON MAN TODAY? The reason there is so much division is because every time someone decides to start a new church, which is not THE TRUE CHURCH, they separate the gifts. These gifts are meant to be a part of THE SAME BODY but now they have very little to do with each other, if anything at all.

The scripture clearly shows that most local assemblies in the first century understood, through correct teachings, that "THE CHURCH WAS SPOKEN INTO EXISTENCE AND FOUNDED BY THE WORD OF GOD, IN THE PERSON OF JESUS", and that it was HIS CHURCH in many different locations.

If we dare deviate from BEING THE CHURCH HE GIVES LIFE TO, we disqualify ourselves from walking IN THE TRUTH, ACCORDING TO HIS DEFINITION OF HIS TRUTH. HE WILL NOT take from us our free will to choose to follow HIS WORD OF TRUTH THAT LEADETH INTO ALLLLLLLL TRUTH. NOR WILL HIS WORD KEEP you from joining yourself to division when you don't ACKNOWLEDGE HIS SPIRIT OF UNITY. Here again is the reason why we emphasize the importance of KNOWING THE WORD OF GOD, EVEN TO BE MADE ONE IN HIM AS WE GIVE OURSELVES TO HIM BY THE ALMIGHTY WORD THAT PRODUCES THE FAITH THAT SUPERSEDES The natural things that change by the wisdom and strength of man.

Let us look at the writings of Bro Paul, who was called and chosen to be "an apostle", one of many. But never did he exalt himself as "THE APOSTLE PAUL". Self-exaltation to be EQUAL TO GOD is the spirit of Lucifer.
When people don't KNOW THE WORD OF GOD, they are unable to draw from HIS SPIRIT THE GRACE AND HUMILITY, TO BE CORRECTED AND RECEIVE FROM ANYONE CARRYING HIS WORD. They're apt to read anything into what they read.

Let's read out of first Corinthians 1:10. Now I beseech you, brethren, by THE NAME OF OUR LORD JESUS CHRIST, that ye all speak the same thing, and that there be "no divisions" among you; but that ye be perfectly joined together in the same mind and in the same judgment."

You "MUST" read on to get the full impact of what Paul was trying to say to THE CHURCH OF GOD which was at Corinth, and to all that CALL UPON THE NAME OF JESUS CHRIST OUR LORD, from the greatest to the least.

I wrote all of that to make my point. If you have given yourself to another version of God's Word and have joined yourself to someone else's church, you're trying to read someone else's mail. Even with the best of intentions to do good, the spirit of deception and division are always the product of not BEING KEPT BY THE SAME POWER THAT UPHOLDS All things, BY THE POWER OF HIS WORD, Not the letter they used to try and kill one another with.

To THE CHURCH OF THE LORD JESUS IN YOUR CITY:

There is enough truth written to point us all to THE SPIRIT WHO CANNOT lie. But, we lie if we know how to quote scripture without KNOWING WHAT HIS SPIRIT IS SAYING. We don't know if HE IS CORRECTING US, SHOWING US that our motives are out of order, or which scripture to use when and for the right reason according to HIS WILL. Who else can judge the motives of the heart?

AS THE LORD SPEAKS TO YOU WHO CAN HEAR, TO LOVE AND OBEY HIM, THE LORD IS YET BUILDING HIS CHURCH TO PERFECT US TO BE ONE IN HIM, UNITED IN HIS KINGDOM and VOID of division! IN HIS GOVERNMENTAL ORDER, HIS

GIFTS ARE NOT ONLY CALLED BUT HAVE
WHOLEHEARTEDLY SOUGHT OUT THE ONE
CALLING THEM, bypassing higher education, bible
school, larger ministries, or the opinion of someone who's
foundation is based on division and the traditions of men.
Knowing there is nothing within them or anyone else to fill
the void Except THE ONE CALLING THEM TO COME
TO HIM! So, like the one out of ten lepers who was
HEALED, He sought THE ONE WHO HAD THE
POWER TO HEAL BY HIS WORD ALONE. Before
going on to anyone, or on with his life, he obeyed THE
SPIRIT OF THE FATHER WHO DRAWS US TO
JESUS, WHO HAS SO MUCH MORE TO GIVE US
THAN HEALING. BUT, THE POWER TO MAKE ONE
WHOLE. AND BE CHOSEN, SUBJECT TO BE
CORRECTED BY HIS WORD, TAUGHT OF THE
LORD, ANOINTED BY HIM, AND SENT TO CARRY
THE WORD OF GOD IN UNITY WITH THE FATHER.
PREACHING JESUS WITH THE POWER OF GOD
AND HIS KINGDOM OF GOD'S LOVE, THE JOY OF
THE LORD, AND THE PEACE OF GOD THAT
SURPASSES human understanding. In realizing the need
for THE CHURCH OF GOD TO ARISE, THE HEAD
WILL GIVE HIS GIFTS,THAT'S ABLE TO WALK
TOGETHER IN THE SPIRIT OF UNITY EMPOWERED
WITH THE LOVE OF GOD TO OVERRIDE any discord
sown by the spirits that hate the very idea of UNITY IN
THE TRUTH IN GOD'S WORD WRITTEN ON OUR
HEARTS. If we, who will CONFESS CHRIST IN
TRUTH, GIVE UP our free will to govern our own lives
by the knowledge of good and evil, HE WILL EMPOWER
US WITH HIS WISDOM, KNOWLEDGE AND
UNDERSTANDING. GRACE AND MERCY TO

FORGIVE IN LONG SUFFERING, POSITIONED TO GIVE HIM ALL THE GLORY FOR WHAT ONLY HE CAN DO. If there is a disagreement on what the scripture says about church doctrine, we have a HIGHER AUTHORITY, THE HEAD OF THE CHUCH, JESUS! It may take time for us to create an atmosphere for HIM TO COME INTO, by our getting on one accord. For someone in the assembly should be able to see past the confusion and remind everyone, THE LORD IS NOT the author of confusion. Outside the governmental order of THE LORD'S CHURCH, men are governed by their knowledge of scriptures alone. When there's a major problem, JESUS, not being the head of someone else's church means their pastor has the final say. If anyone happens to HEAR FROM GOD on the matter, what he or she hears had better line up with the one man in charge or they might be instructed to find another church, or start one of their own. For example: If a person with the gift of healing decides to leave and start their own church, their segregated church ministry would be based on healing. The same with deliverance, fire baptism or baptism in Jesus' Name in natural water. Using Jesus' Name is not justification for promoting division! WHEN THE SPIRIT OF UNITY WOULD HAVE US ALL BE BAPIZED IN HIS NAME, HIS SPIRIT, HIS WORD, THE FATHER, THE SON AND THE HOLY GHOST, WISDOM, KNOWLEDGE AND UNDERSTANDING, MERCY, GRACE, TRUTH AND RIGHTEOUSNESS, LOVE, JOY, AND PEACE IN THE HOLY GHOST. Look at all the divided opposing fundamental bible based groups, the separated prosperity groups, the full gospel groups, holiness groups, and faith groups. All the different denominations, non-denominations, all the other organizations not mentioned.

Nothing personal, but there are too many separated groups out there for me to mention, but you get the point. Everybody's church takes on the flavor of the leader and the people are not satisfied and don't know why they go from church to church trying to find their place. If the gift that feeds your Spirit best is not in the house and you're only receiving from pastors, then that is the reason why. Some of the larger congregations are being fed by an Apostle and everyone in the congregation receives something. That doesn't excuse division and is still not the church the world will someday see when all the TRUE GIFTS OF GOD WILL BE SUBMITTED TO THE UNITY OF THE SPIRIT OF GOD.

HIS SOVEREIGN WORD COMMANDS UNITY IN HIS KINGDOM AND IN HIS CHURCH. Remember HIS GOVERNING ORDER OF Apostles; and Prophets; Evangelists; and Pastors and Teachers; For the PERFECTING of the saints, for the work of the ministry, for the edifying of THE BODY OF CHRIST:
Till we all COME IN THE UNITY OF THE FAITH, AND OF THE KNOWLEDGE OF THE SON OF GOD, UNTO A PERFECT MAN, UNTO THE MEASURE OF THE STATURE OF THE FULNESS OF CHRIST.

If I was in the position of "a" pastor and allowed people to call me "THE PASTOR." I would have two options: The first and wisest decision would be to seek THE LORD FOR HIS GRACE AND MERCY. And A HEART TO HEAR AND RECEIVE HIS WORD TO OBEY HIS WILL. What a witness to the world and everyone out of order, for someone whose name is as popular as JESUS. (According to world advertisement) What if they TRULY

HUMBLE themselves and show the world how to repent, BEFORE THE FATHER OF THOSE WHO WILL OBEY HIM. HE IS SEARCHING FOR those who will worship HIM IN SPIRIT AND IN TRUTH, for THE SPIRIT OF TRUTH KNOWS those who are subject to HIS SPIRIT and who will be led by the flesh. Whose name is exalted in the church you know? Do they understand JESUS did not PREACH THE KINGDOM OF OUR FATHER while joined to a Spirit of organized religious division? Whatever name people give the government to become legal, their church is illegal IN THE KINGDOM OF OUR FATHER.

If I were you, and caught up in the bondage of a man-made church. (Not mentioned in your bible or mine). I would honestly "pray" that GOD WOULD HAVE MERCY ON me and deliver me from ever learning, and leaning on my own understanding but instead to come INTO THE FULL KNOWLEDGE OF HIM, THE TRUTH. GOD LOVES US SO MUCH HE WOULD TELL US THE TRUTH if we are SEEKING HIM WITH OUR WHOLE HEART and are open to receive FROM HIM even if HE USES someone our natural mind would rather not hear from. And, in the natural, the one HE CHOOSES TO TELL THE TRUTH they, too, would think that you were someone they would rather not approach. But, thank GOD FOR HIS LOVE RECEIVED IN OUR HEARTS, THAT ENPOWERS US TO MOVE PAST what we might think to BE MOVED BY THE SPIRIT. Then we can't help but compel others to come INTO THE UNITY OF THE TRUTH. It's recorded that we would KNOW THE TRUTH AND THE TRUTH WOULD SET US FREE.

ALSO, WHOM THE SON SETS FREE IS "FREE INDEED"!

As a witness of THE TRUTH, you will meet a lot of people, some will confess to KNOW JESUS, but as you try and find FELLOWSHIP IN THE SPIRIT OF GOD'S WORD they're offended. When hearing that THE WORD OF GOD IS GOD, and they've been taught all their lives the bible is the word of god. You must allow THE SPIRIT OF WISDOM AND GRACE TO GIVE you what to say. And put yourself in their shoes. You may be the only one to sow THE SEED OF GOD'S WORD UNTO THEM in such a way that HE CAN BE RECEIVED, and can't easily be shaken when you separate. You already know their position is to challenge anyone that disagrees with their private interpretations of the only word they can see. But your prayer is THAT OUR FATHER WOULD SEND someone across their path to WATER THE SEED sown.

Preacher or no preacher, HIS WORD IS SEARCHING the hearts of all people, TO BRING THEM INTO HIS KINGDOM OF UNITY IN HIM.

Aren't you glad THE TRUTH IS FREE AND HE PAID THE FULL PRICE FOR us to freely RECEIVE OF HIS SPIRIT ALL THAT IS ETERNAL without money? THE TRUE WORD OF GOD IS OUR CREATOR, not another version. And money can't buy HIM.

In order for us to get back to THE ONLY TRUE FOUNDATION, we must understand the purpose of the gifts JESUS GAVE ON HIS WAY BACK TO THE FATHER.

43

As you probably know, our five fingers are like the five gifts and the thumb being the strongest is able to touch every other finger on the hand with ease. Even so with the Apostles, and the Prophets point THE WAY and working together we ALL MUST NOT FORGET WHO THE HEAD IS AND GIVE HIM THE OPTION TO USE WHOEVER HE SO CHOOSES. Our maturity will be evident in our ability to submit to one another "AS WE SUBMIT UNTO THE LORD". The middle finger represents the Evangelists which can reach farther and will allow the Apostles and Prophets to come in a city or a House of Prayer for all people, subject TO THE SPIRIT OF TRUTH TO establish the work ON THE ONLY TRUE ETERNAL FOUNDATION, JESUS, GOD'S OWN WORD and THE MASTER BUILDER. Then HE, THE SPIRIT, CAN USE HIS APPOINTED GIFTS TO SET IN PLACE Under-shepherds and Teachers and all the other gifts will find their place because their gifts will make room for them, ALL ACCORDING TO THE LEADING OF THE LORD OF COURSE. Scripture properly interpreted points this out. Now, if an Evangelist gives up his office to become The Pastor, it's out of order. Likewise any gift out of order that will try and exalt themselves to the position of THE APOSTLE or THE PROPHET OR THE EVANGELIST, THE PASTOR OR THE TEACHER, THAT IS JESUS POSITION. And THAT'S WHY there is so much ungodly division and confusion. Men and Women positioned as to be equal to JESUS! And, without an ear to be corrected by THE WORD OF THE LORD OR ANYONE else outside there out of place organized miss-understanding. Having a wrong foundation could lead to the equivalent of allowing a farmer, a landscaper, a mailman, a baby sitter and a first grade teacher to do heart surgery on people. You must ask yourself what happened to submitting to one another in love. My little finger works just fine with its function as my little finger and not my thumb or first finger. An apostle may have a primary gift of a teacher or one of the others, but he is not the whole hand. What damage we will do to the forces of darkness when our hands are used to speak to the deaf and with our hands speak to the blind. AND THE HEAD COMMANDS THE fingers to come together and form a fist to really do some damage to the enemy, when our fingers apart were only slapping at an enemy that is out to steel, kill and destroy! IF WE DON'T KNOW THE SPIRIT OF TRUTH, how will we know the spirit of deception?

If I was the head of a traditional church and read this book, the first thing I would do is to ask GOD'S FORGIVENESS and allow HIM TO LEAD. We all have gone astray MUST come to a place of repentance. But we have the advantage of looking at men like Saul who was CONVERTED to Paul, a prime example OF THE POWER GOD HAS TO MAKE HIMSELF KNOWN to a heart tired of being on the wrong road headed in the wrong direction. AND, THE GLORY OUR FATHER WILL GET OUT OF TAKING a person humbled from one extreme to HEIGHTS UNKNOWN AND PEACE WITH OUR FATHER FOREVER. For as long as you're divided I must ask the question, FATHER WHAT CAN I DO? In your shoes I would then take as long as it takes to seek GODS FACE until HE REVEALS HIMSELF TO me, the rest will be history according to how THE LORD LEADS YOU IN RIGHTEOUSNESS AND TRUTH.

Get to KNOW HIS VOICE FOR HIS WORD IS IN ALL TRUTH AND RIGHTEOUSNESS. Remember reading that HIS SHEEP WILL "KNOW HIS VOICE" and another they will not follow. Some of you, who will humble yourselves, could be exalted and given the gift of a servant of all or an apostle or prophet and you may only need to set the proper gifts in their right position. I know of a prophet who told an apostle what his gift was and that's a big part of how I came to write this book. Otherwise, I might still be sitting under someone, frustrated to high heavens unable to know my purpose or use it in their church because NO one out ranks the pastor. BUT, IN THE KINGDOM OF OUR HEAVENLY FATHER, THERE'S ROOM FOR ALL THE GIFTS HE GIVES FOR THE PURPOSE HE GAVE THEM. For, if you receive a prophet in the name of a prophet, you will receive the reward of a prophet and be OPEN TO GOD'S WORD. The scriptures are not only to be read but to be experienced in about the same way the writers EXPERIENCED THE WORD OF GOD AND WERE CHANGED AND MADE ONE IN JESUS. If CHRIST BE IN YOU, SO IS HIS WORD. If you know about HIM or read about HIM, your heart turned towards HIM is all you need. No longer can we jump over scripture designed to help bring us INTO THE UNITY OF THE SPIRIT or reduce correction down to what was meant for only those to whom the letters where addressed! No scripture is meant for any private interpretation. Here again is a safe guard when all the gifts are in operation in a CITY CHURCH GOVERNED BY GOD AND SUBMITTED TO ONE ANOTHER. Men might turn the pages of scripture or suggest something totally outside His Will. But, THE WORD OF THE LORD WILL STAND FOR EVER WHICH no man can change. HE, unlike the book, KNOWS the Hearts of all men. There's no escaping THE ALMIGHTY, ALL KNOWING, LIVING FATHER WHO CARES.

God used Paul to deal with division in the church which was at Corinth. You've read the letter before but hopefully it will take on a more personal meaning as will all the scriptures understanding their purpose. Let me say this while I'm on the subject: consider praise and worship, thanksgiving and prayer. Without us trying to explain what the writer meant or how to do it scripturally, why not in coming together, worship and praise Him in your own unique way. In our obedience to unity is love for one another. With patience the Head of the Church will give us a clear Word through one of His gifts – a Word to unite the whole Church -- Who in turn can get on with our Father's business of reaching the world with the gospel of the LORD JESUS Christ and His Kingdom.

Ok. What did Paul say to the Church at Corinth? I Corinthians 1: 9-10.
Now, you must understand HE's writing to the whole Church at Corinth. Verse 2 reads, "Unto the church of God, to them that are sanctified in Christ JESUS. . ." He's addressing everyone who hears or reads this letter: Verses 11-17. Here again is a good message for our time for all the division about baptism today. But we've taken division to a whole different level over everything we can imagine. That's why the LORD'S CHURCH IN your city

must understand and work toward unity in the church – HIS CHURCH.

Paul continues in Verses 25 to 29. Dropping down to Chapter 3, we read Verses 1 to 11. We've covered in earlier chapters how in the beginning was the Word and the Word was with God and the Word was God. All things were made by Him and without Him was not anything made that was made. That's exactly how we must accomplish whatever HE HAS for us to do. Separately or together as THE BODY, we can do nothing without HIM.

We're all called to be ONE IN HIM where there's no envying or taking a position of lording over your brothers and sisters, for that's who we really are, having THE SAME HEAVENLY FATHER. Whenever THE CHURCH OF OUR LORD come TOGETHER TO BE THE CHURCH, we can know that HE WILL BE IN THE MIDST AND HIS BLESSING IS WITH HIM.

Let us not give up acknowledging THE KINGDOM OF GOD for fear of losing a man-made building. When HE HAS THE POWER IN HIS CREATIVE WORD OF WISDOM TO GIVE THE CHURCH BOTH. HE can make us whole as soon as our hearts are turned toward HIM TO FOLLOW HIM! Will you be willing to give up your building to THE CHURCH JESUS IS BUILDING? HE SAID BLESSED ARE THE MEEK FOR THEY SHALL INHERIT THE EARTH. That beats any man-made. Make it A TRUE HOUSE OF PRAYER FOR ALL PEOPLE ACCORDING TO THE DIRECTION OF THE HOLY SPIRIT, not a man-made organization out of GOD'S ORDER OF GOVERNING HIS CHURCH.

Remember, GOD'S GOVERNMENTAL ORDER IN HIS CHURCH. If you are not an Apostle or A Prophet, pray that GOD would send them across your path, submitted to one another. If they are TRUE TO THE FAITH, they will not do you harm but will be a blessing unto you beyond your wildest expectations. For HE that would be the greatest among you shall be your Servant which would be like JESUS, WHO HUMBLED HIMSELF FROM GOD DOWN TO MAN AND FROM MAN TO THE SERVANT OF ALL.

Here again, we seek HIS SPIRIT TO MAKE ALIVE THE TRUTH BEHIND what was written. When we acknowledge THE ONLY WORD OF GOD IS GOD, we will understand GOD IS NOT LIMITED by 66 books or 6,000 books. Read or re-read John 21:25 and there are also many other things which JESUS DID which, if everyone had been written, I suppose that even the world itself could not have contained the books that should be written. Amen. Don't get sidetracked behind any confusion in the letter or our modern day translations. Because our dependence is on THE SPIRIT not in our understanding, the things of the spirit of division, confusion and misunderstanding that would have us divided should be put on the back burner. FOR THE SPIRIT MIGHT BE TEACHING US PATIENCE, LOVE AND HOW TO FORGIVE others as you would have HIM FORGIVE you. FOR, HIS MERCIES ARE NEW EVERY MORNING.

Once more, the problem I have with people calling the Bible (any version), the Word of God is they haven't EXPERIENCED THE ALMIGHTY POWER AND GLORY OF THE ONLY TRUE LIFE GIVING

CREATIVE ONLY INFALLABLE WORD OF GOD, TO KNOW THERE IS NONE OTHER BESIDE HIM WHO GIVES WISDOM TO the simple!

Again, let's deal with the root of the problem. Most people walk in error following all kinds of voices by not KNOWING THE TRUTH found only IN THE WORD OF GOD GIVEN THE NAME JESUS, NOT James.

This natural world is changing so fast. If you are not founded upon THE SOLID ROCK, you can easily be swept away with the limited earthly knowledge of men who have chosen religion to be their choice of a good business career.

Chapter Five

Foundation, Foundation, Foundation

When I was young, back in the 40's and 50's they had a toy for boys called "The Joe Palooka Punching Bag". It stood about 4 feet and every time you punched it, it would go down and come right back up. The reason was because at the base of the plastic image of the rubber boxer was something fixed that was heavy enough to cause the balloon to always come back up in an upright position. No matter how hard or how often it was hit, it would always come right back up. So it is with the believer whose foundation is on THE SURE FOUNDATION OF GOD'S OWN INFALLIBLE WORD. IN KNOWING HIM, THERE WOULD BE NO DOUBT AS TO WHAT HE SAYS FOR HIS PURPOSE WILL MANIFEST ITSELF IN whoever or TO whatever HE SPEAKS. HE MADE HIS OWN ETERNAL INFALLIBLE WORD FLESH, GAVE HIS WORD A NAME AND HE, BEING IN THE FORM OF A MAN, GAVE CLEAR UNDERSTANDING TO WHAT HE SAID AND WHAT HE MEANT, WRITTEN ON their hearts while their heads tried to comprehend the things that were not natural.

You do know you can repeat what someone says Word for Word and yet, not really know what they mean. One of the greatest problems people face today is their need for more knowledge rather than to HUMBLE themselves and be RECEIVED BY THE SOURCE OF ALL TRUTH, WISDOM, KNOWLEDGE, AND REVELATION, and EVEN LIFE FOREVER MORE.

People love all THE PROMISES OF GOD WRITTEN and pursue them rather than SEEKING FIRST THE KING AND HIS KINGDOM. The thing about a King is you don't get to choose on what terms you serve Him, unlike people who think they can serve GOD in the way they so choose, or in the custom of the divided religious group they so choose.

This next statement should be an eye opener: For, if OUR CREATOR doesn't give you eyes to see and ears to hear, you can meet all the religious requirements your divided group requires to be a leader, and still not KNOW THE ONE we're all suppose to FOLLOW.

CALL ON THE LORD UNTIL HE ANSWERS YOU. FOR HE IS ALIVE AND HE IS STILL THE SAME AS HE WAS when men TOUCHED HIM AND WERE HEALED. Some people who had a need and who cried from the bottom of their hearts, without shame, would not be denied. Like blind Bartimaeus, a man you may have read about (Mark 10:46-52), no man can come to JESUS except THE FATHER DRAWS them. Nor can anyone come unto THE FATHER EXCEPT THROUGH JESUS. And you should know that's BY HIS SPIRIT, not the flesh.

So, what is THE SPIRIT SAYING? Let's look at a very, very important scripture written by one of his followers (Romans 10). Misinterpreted, you will be led to think man is your source. **FAITH COMETH ALIVE BY HEARING AND HEARING BY THE WORD OF GOD WHO SPEAKS. Preachers sent will always point others to JESUS WHO IS SPEAKING IN UNLIMITED WAYS

SEARCHING the hearts, and GIVING to those to whom HE GAVE THE ABILITY "TO HEAR HIM". Then our faith, MARRIED TO HIS FAITH, ENABLES US TO SAY WHAT HE SAYS even in the face of a world of misunderstanding, confusion, deception and the results of not being able to HEAR HIM SPEAK THE TRUTH consistently, nor see beyond the natural world that's governed by the many voices that lie.

One major key overlooked is that GOD GIVES people THE ABILITY TO HEAR. Let's look at it this way. In man's quest to draw people to them, they're interpretation is more like: faith comes by hearing them; most of Whom just "went", not "sent" so they think they are "the pastor" resulting in their followers acknowledging them as "the" pastor, unable to HEAR and OBEY WHAT THE GOOD SHEPHERD SAYS because HE contradicts the perpetrator Who is the founder and the Head of His Church and the final authority of His own Word interpreted ever so cunningly, some unknowingly to lead the deaf and dumb into bondage up under him or her. Religious bondage is bondage of the worst kind. If you can't break FREE, you must be SET FREE.

For the proud self-exalted leaders who might reject THE SPIRIT OF TRUTH WHEN HE is acknowledged, there is but one way out. They must humble themselves and receive REVELATION FROM GOD. Opposed to educated knowledge about HIM, many preach King James or another version as their foundation, not KING JESUS AS THE WORD OF GOD. What a testimony unto all that know them, to actually see them fulfill Philippians 2:5 that reads "Let this mind be in you, which was also in CHRIST JESUS".

Here's a side note that needs to be repeated: When a person's foundation is clearly rooted in division (whatever name they give it), look how foolish it is to think THE SPIRIT OF TRUTH is subject to move according to their dysfunction. Being in bondage to the dictates of the Spirit of division they, too, must become transparent before all and yield themselves unto JESUS along with all the world no matter what position or status they think they have.

The REDEEMING NEWS is this: the lower anyone goes in acknowledging THE SOVEREIGNTY OF THE LIVING WORD, the higher HE is able to raise them up. And, no matter what position we end up IN HIM, WE WILL BE COMPLETELY SATISFIED "IN HIM"! ETERNALLY GRATEFUL AND KEPT BY THE POWER OF HIS WORD TO WHOM WE GIVE PRAISE WITH JOY UNSPEAKABLE AND FULL OF GLORY THAT COMES FROM HIM WHO KNOWS HIS OWN. And, ON TOP OF THAT, HE GIVES US ACCESS INTO HIS GLORIOUS KINGDOM, BY HIS WORD WHO SPEAKS TO He who has an ear to HEAR HIM. Even today!! For this is the day that THE LORD HAS MADE.

Let's look at GOD'S GOVERNMENTAL ORDER again FROM HIS PERSPECTIVE. We have all been deceived at some time in thinking we could be joined to someone else's church and reap THE BENEFITS SET IN PLACE BY THE WORD OF GOD FOR HIS CHURCH.

Now, if you think that because men have the title of Reverend, Doctor, Bishop, Pastor, Founder and the Head of something he or she named, organized and has permission from the government to be legal with a tax identification number is the same church JESUS SAID HE WOULD BUILD, you have another thought coming. Then, if you think the same way, you need your head examined. Then, if you still think the same way, you're just crazy or flat out nuts.

JESUS, THE ALMIGHTY WORD OF GOD MADE FLESH, GAVE HIS LIFE IN THE BIRTHING PROCESS for those BORN THROUGH HIS LIVING WATER AND HIS REDEEMING BLOOD, which the carnal mind can't fully comprehend.

Do you HEAR WHAT I HEAR? If you hear and know King James only and someone you are trying to walk together with LEARNED TO KNOW KING JESUS how do you expect to ever agree? Because some people can't HEAR THE VOICE OF THE LORD, they may find it hard to believe others can. THE BENEFITS OF BEING A TRUE REPERSENTATIVE OF THE KINGDOM OF OUR FATHER IS that we get to REVERENCE THE KING OF KINGS AS MATURE SONS WITH ALL THE RIGHTS INHERITED BY THE WHOLE FAMILY IN HEAVEN AND IN EARTH. We get to INHERIT AND EXPERIENCE ETERNAL LIFE. OUR MOTIVES ARE CHANGED and THE OBVIOUS -- OUR LANGUAGE CHANGES.

People in the natural operate on levels, but when THE LORD DELIVERS us to see from THE KINGDOM

VIEWPOINT, we can see the limitations of every earthly dominion. But, for them to see and TRULY UNDERSTAND where you're coming from, they can't. They're limited to earthly visible knowledge that's subject to change by the intellect of man. When we are TRANSFORMED BY EXPERIENCING HIM AND BECOME A conduit for THE WORD OF GOD WHO GIVES US WHAT TO SAY, (if we're listening) we find FELLOWSHIP IN AND THROUGH HIM.

We say what HE SAYS and others don't have THE FAITH THAT COMES FROM HEARING him. So, they're too weak to speak contrary to the fruits of organized division and traditional religion.

"Please give JESUS HIS CHURCH back":

People give their lives to JESUS and before they are able to HEAR, KNOW, LOVE, OBEY AND FOLLOW HIM, they're taken away into some type of religious bondage. A man-made organization where men even call their divided groups the "church" and the building they purchased with a set dollar amount. And, in bondage to the lenders, they call it, and sometimes the people, the "church" when they mix in a word of truth.

Have you ever thought, or maybe not, what you have to give up when you join someone else's church other than the one you were born again into or the one someone told you that you were born again into?

You give up the right to ACKNOWLEDGE JESUS AS THE TRUE PASTOR WHO WATCHES OVER HIS

SHEEP BOTH DAY AND NIGHT. BUT, the men or women you acknowledge as "the Pastor" have no clue as to your purpose or why THE CREATOR MADE YOU in the first place, nor are they able to keep you from falling or give you LIFE ETERNAL.

How can anyone ENTER INTO HIS KINGDOM IF they don't RECEIVE HIS WORD, aren't subject TO HIS WORD OF TRUTH, AND CANNOT BE CORRECTED BY HIS SAVING WORD OF LOVE? IT'S BY HIS WORD HE GIVES us PERMISSION TO ENTER INTO THE KINGDOM.

How can you have an ear to hear, know and obey JESUS' VOICE TO "HIS CHURCH" if you're only open to a word for another's church you've joined yourself to and purposed to be faithful to and not another?

This explains when men don't enter in through THE DOOR WHEN JESUS IS THAT DOOR. They try and climb up some other way as a thief or a robber who doesn't have a problem trying to lay hold to ALL THE PROMISES OF GOD, avoiding having to give their whole heart to THE ONE WHO KNOWS THE DIFFERENCE between wholehearted and halfhearted, Carnal and SPIRITUAL. BELIEVE this: HE IS GREATER THAN man's misinterpretations they only debate about in scriptures. If a person is not TRANSFORMED AND CONVERTED BY OUR LIFESOURCE, they can easily settle for the word of men and women and never consider the difference in man's word about GOD AND GOD'S WORD TO MAN.

Some divided groups believe GOD only SPEAKS IN A STILL SMALL VOICE SO they want nothing to do with people who are loud and exceedingly joyful. On the other side of that, the loud people don't want anything to do with the quiet and reserved folk. Our solution is to RECEIVE THE WORD OF GOD AND gain ACCESS BY HIM INTO HIS KINGDOM void of the pettiness. The spirit of deception is known for trying to keep THE LORD'S CHURCH FROM BEING THE CHURCH. You do remember reading what happened WHEN GOD HAD Moses bring the people to the foot of the mountain. How the whole mountain shook when HE DID SPEAK and their response was fear! Then, they told Moses he could HEAR FROM GOD and then tell them WHAT GOD SAID.

We cannot limit HIM FROM SPEAKING ANY WAY HE SO PLEASES. So, don't be like the religious leaders of old who could not receive THE ALMIGHTY WORD OF GOD IN THE FORM OF A MAN even with all their knowledge of the scriptures that they had at the time. Now that we know of THE TRUE FOUNDATION, let us go on to KNOW HIM BY HIS WORD.

CHAPTER Six

GLORY TO GOD IN THE HIGHEST.

Let it be known to all the earth in every way possible, THE GOD AND FATHER AND CREATOR OF ALL THE UNIVERSE IS WORTHY OF ALL THE GLORY AND HONOR we can give and more. All the reverence, respect, and worship and praise every created being can give HIM from eternity to ETERNITY.

From generation to generation, the knowledge of OUR LOVING FATHER has been known and there will be someone to give GLORY TO GOD IN THE HIGHEST IN KNOWING IN WHOM THEY HAVE BELIEVED UNTIL HE MADE HIMSELF KNOWN.

For the truth to be told, the greatest thing anyone can obtain is A RIGHT RELATIONSHIP WITH OUR LIFE SOURCE. To know about HIM from the knowledge of others is not what I mean, but to KMOW HIM IN AN EXPERIENTIAL, INTIMATE WAY would better explain what I'm trying to say. And yet, if this whole book was designed to explain in our earthly words using every word in the dictionary, I would still come up short in giving you the EXPERIENCE OF OUR CREATOR. I AM THAT I AM, IS ALL THAT HE IS.

HE is not just limited to the many names we call HIM. From our translations FOR HE "IS" LOVE; HE "IS" JOY; HE "IS" PEACE; HE "IS" OUR POWER AND OUR SALVATION, NOT to be debated. For many fall from GRACE by yielding to the spirit of the enemy that keeps them unwisely divided about scriptures on SALVATION. Bro David let it be known that HE HAS BECOME MY SALVATION. To them that KNOW HIM HE IS ALSO THE ANSWER TO ALL OUR PRAYERS.

In all of that, you still have to EXPERIENCE HIM for yourself to truly know what I mean when your intellect might settle for analyzing and debating about what was said without ever asking and receiving from the author just what HE meant. What one means and what one says can be interpreted in as many ways as you have bible believing, divided groups, all doing their own thing in the same city, and all with a different interpretation of what others' experienced and wrote about which now has become big business.

THE GLORY OF GOD IS IN THE FACT THAT HE IS THE FINAL AUTHORITY OF WHAT EVER HE SAYS, down to every jot and tittle. HE EVEN KNOWS the mindset of the subjects HE USED to echo into the earth realm what they heard from THE ORIGINAL AUTHOR HIMSELF. When people don't know HIS VOICE they don't KNOW OR HONOR HIS WORD.

Many people can strive and claim to master the many different versions of scripture. But, can you imagine what the world would be like if man had been given the final authority of THE ALMIGHTY WORD OF GOD?

It's bad enough with men thinking THE CREATOR OF THE WHOLE UNIVERSE, "HE", THE LIVING WORD OF GOD could be subject to the limited, earthly divided interpretations and the thoughts of men and women. If the created being were to instruct THE CREATOR, then THE SPIRIT OF TRUTH would have to become subject to the spirit of error, and THE SPIRIT OF LOVE would have no power over hate.

THE SPIRIT OF UNITY would be powerless to make us ONE IN HIM and THE KINGDOM OF HEAVEN would be as divided as what most demonstrate from Sunday to Sunday.

If THE ALMIGHTY WORD OF GOD WAS in the hands of religious leaders today that same spirit would have HIM CRUCIFIED all over again. For, if you think my words are strong, what if you had to hear HIM SAY "DEPART FROM ME YE WORKERS OF INIQUITY"?

A person can't be rooted in deception and division then by mixing their private interpretations with some written truths think they are justified by all the good works they do. Maybe I misinterpreted Matthew 7:21-29.

Satan, the deceiver and Father of lies gave Adam's bride another version of what GOD SAID. We cannot be so foolish again to be subject to that age old lie. If she would have HEARD GOD FIRST HAND for herself she too would have been so full of what GOD SAID AND THE LIFE OF WHAT HE MEANT that she like Adam could not have been deceived. We too must come to not only know what someone said about what GOD SAID, BUT we MUST KNOW HIM FOR OURSELVES. For the BENEFITS OF HAVING A RELATIONSHIP WITH OUR HEAVENLY FATHER IS OUR GOAL, and is far richer than being accepted by the religious groups that so earnestly, religiously advertise for more memberships for their Church. Remember, anything you can join, you can quit. But, remember also what JESUS, the Word of God made flesh, said: you must be born again INTO THE FAMILY OF OUR FATHER.

When people don't KNOW THE VALUE OF BEING BORN INTO THE FAMILY OF GOD they will do like Isaac and sell their birthright for a bowl of beans or join something they can't get out of.

Instead of being the church JESUS gave birth to, they join someone else's church, ever learning to receive praise of men when they should have EARS TO HEAR, RECEIVE AND BELIEVE WHAT THE LORD IS SAYING TO HAVE A WORD OF LIFE TO GIVE the many people they meet every day who don't KNOW WHO JESUS IS.

IN OUR FATHER'S KINGDOM, WE ARE SUBJECT TO HIS SPIRIT OF TRUTH AND RIGHTEOUSNESS ABOVE what we see, hear or feel from the forces outside. FOR HE CAN CREATE AND MAKE WHAT WAS MEANT FOR evil TURN AROUND FOR OUR GOOD AND HIS PURPOSES TO PREVAIL.

Questions & Answers:

The Questions given have one answer each. They are designed to help you think from THE KINGDOM PERSPECTIVE void of deception, misunderstanding, and to be fully aware that THE WORD OF THE KING IS NOT the author of confusion. And HE is not responsible for us being double minded.

Your best source for the answers to any of life's questions is THE SPIRIT OF TRUTH. As you learn to HEAR, KNOW, LOVE AND OBEY HIS VOICE, HE WILL LEAD YOU INTO ALL TRUTH FOUND IN HIMSELF. HIS ALMIGHTY WORD WILL KEEP YOU, Not you keep HIM like men keep the letter, so they think, in following the spirit of division and error.

The purpose of these questions is to make sure your answers are based on THE ONLY SURE FOUNDATION THAT'S ETERNAL. CHRIST JESUS BEING THAT FOUNDATION ESTABLISHED BEFORE THE WORLD WAS CREATED.

Other sources would be other believers, different bible versions. Keep in mind that bibles are sometimes subject to reveal the beliefs of the copyright holder without the reader even being aware. Find out who owns the copyrights and better understand its spirit. The library is a good source for commentaries on the bibles.

1. Who was Adam's first conversation with in the garden?
2. Is Satan subject to obey the letter or THE SPIRIT OF GOD?
3. Can Satan quote scripture with hidden motives cunning enough to
   deceive people today?
4. Which divided group or groups today would be the equivalent of the
   divided religious leaders of old?
5. What IN HEAVEN can money buy?
6. What in the earth realm cannot be sold?
7. WILL JESUS FIND FAITH ON THE EARTH?

Using your preferred translation of scripture, read Genesis 1:1.

How many times God said: over & over and over, how the emphasis was placed on "God said". So we see OUR CREATOR HAS THE POWER TO SPEAK BEFORE HE MADE MAN. Moses learned about CREATION FROM GOD, not the first Adam's writings. Men had to learn how to read and write after the fall. But EVERYTHING GOD SAYS MANIFESTS AND OBEYS HIS WORD, everything but man's free will that GOD DID NOT TAKE from him. We come to know about HIM by the testimony of others, but we come to "KNOW HIM" BY HIM CHOOSING US. WHAT IS THE SPIRIT OF OUR LORD ASKING YOU TO DO TO BE CHOSEN? Wouldn't everyone like to KNOW THE ONE WHO DIED FOR THE SINS OF THE WHOLE WORLD, MAKING IT POSSIBLE FOR US TO BE REDEEMED?

FOR SURE OUR FATHER AND HIS WORD ARE ONE. THE WORD OF GOD IS GOD! Any Word that is not God is not THE WORD OF GOD. Did you know that the Word of God is Spirit and Truth when men receive a WORD FROM GOD and try to convert their experience into writing what's missing? Ask Eve who received second-hand information from a man without sin. When anyone tries to explain THE THUTH in writing, their writing is subject to be misinterpreted and, if it is visible, before too long a price tag is attached and that Word then becomes a product worth the price set by the copyright holder.

Man tried to put a price on THE WORD OF GOD MADE FLESH and the person ended up committing suicide. Everything that can be seen is subject to change and a dollar amount is usually somehow associated with it. BUT, THE SPIRIT IS ETERNAL AND EVERYTHING IN HIM.

A lot of people know a lot about the different aspects OF GOD from an intellectual point of view, but they don't KNOW THE ONE THE NAME JESUS WAS GIVEN TO FOR HE IS SPIRIT AND TRUTH THAT LEADETH INTO ALL TRUTH. When people don't KNOW HIS VOICE, OR CONFESS HIM FOR WHO HE IS, they're subject to their own limited understanding of something they can see, something that's subject to change with the stroke of a pen. Something man's hands have handled.

When the scripture interpreted correctly reads: "Let every man be a liar, but let GOD BE TRUE". SO, we must LEARN TO SAY WHAT HE SAYS. We are to help people be free to receive from OUR FATHER AND FOLLOW HIM AS HE SO CHOOSES TO LEAD. We all "must" be TAUGHT OF HIM. When HE uses us it must be made very, very clear that HE is our SHEPHERD and we altogether must FOLLOW HIM.

I am just your brother and I have no heaven or hell to put anyone in. I am not your HEAVENLY FATHER. I can't keep you and you can't keep me from being FREE! Anyone who has the gift of a Pastor, is an under shepherd, not your GOD. They may be a chief under shepherd, but an under shepherd nonetheless. For THE CHIEF SHEPHERD IS "JESUS".

There is no sound writing for man being the head of THE CHURCH JESUS SAID HE WOULD BUILD OF PEOPLE HE GAVE HIS LIFE FOR AND ROSE UP FROM THE DEAD.

For every known divided religious group able to have their own copyright version changed ever so slightly but just enough to be able to claim copyrights. Have you not read how the letter killeth but THE SPIRIT MAKETH ALIVE? THAT'S WHY OUR FOUNDATION MUST BE ON THE LIFE-GIVING WORD OF GOD HIMSELF.

People walking in the flesh are limited to the things of the earth realm -- earthly knowledge. People walking in THE SPIRIT OF GOD learn to say what HE SAYS AND ALL OF HEAVEN WILL BACK HIS WORD.

Chapter Seven

A Wrong Foundation

THE THINGS RECORDED THAT JESUS SAID WILL MAKE US LOOK TO A HIGHER SOURCE FOR THE ANSWERS. EVEN WHEN HE MADE THINGS PLAIN, WE STILL NEED TO BE CONNECTED TO THE SPIRIT IN ORDER TO FOLLOW HIM AND NOT JUST THE LETTER. I will try and explain: Sometimes people can get so engrossed in leading they forget they too are to FOLLOW. It's recorded in 1st Cor. 3:11, "For no other foundation can anyone lay than that which is laid, which is Jesus Christ". Our Bible is one of the most valuable earthly items we can possess but it must be used for the right purpose. For in it we learn that THE FATHER PLACED NOTHING ABOVE HIS NAME BUT HIS WORD. Now, how you define GOD'S WORD will determine what you place above HIS NAME. Can I suggest to everyone, to do a word study on the "WORD" to see if there is any justification for calling any Bible THE ONLY INFALLABLE WORD OF GOD? If you are not familiar with your bible turn to the concordance usually in the back of most Christian versions. The first Adam's decision to go along with another's version of the Word of God cost them everything. What it costs people today is something they have never known: THE KINGDOM OF HEAVEN, IS ABOVE everything this world has to offer. JESUS' MESSAGE WAS CONSISTENTLY THE SAME FOR YEARS while men followed HIM, GOD IN THE FLESH and they did not understand HIS MESSAGE OF THE KINGDOM AND did not KNOW WHO HE REALLY

67

WAS. BUT, WHEN THEY WERE FILLED WITH HIS HOLY SPIRIT THEY PREACHED JESUS IN SEASON AND OUT. This may read somewhat strange, but is there any bible version referencing King James as being THE WORD OF GOD? Then, let's not try and make it something it cannot possibly be. Could it be that people are deceived and don't know it by giving all the glory and honor to their knowledge and interpretations of the letters and testimonies of others translated thousands and thousands of times over?

In short, if King James is keeping you, give Him or "it" all the glory. But, if you can see the cover being removed off the deceiver and you can HEAR THE SPIRIT OF TRUTH, IT IS HE THAT MADE YOU FREE FROM the religious fallen spirits that lie, not your knowledge of your bible or the theology of the group that best fits the human side of your reasoning.

The message in the four GOSPELS remains the same and instead of getting A REAL UNDERSTANDING OF WHAT WAS RECORDED THAT JESUS SAID, people jump over to what they can better understand in the epistles and learn to teach others the bible. AGAIN AND AGAIN AND AGAIN, THE EARLY CHURCH PREACHED JESUS SO MUCH SO that most of the religious world hated them like they hated THE ONE THAT CALLED THEM, CHOSE THEM, TAUGHT THEM, CORRECTED THEM, ANOINTED AND SENT THEM. They did not preach division in King James BUT UNITY IN THE WORD OF GOD. THE ONLY WORD OF GOD THEY KNEW WAS THE ONE DRILLED INTO THEIR HEADS UNTIL THEIR HEARTS

CAUGHT ON FIRE. What you're HEARING and seeing is not a dream but THE LOVE OF GOD FOR YOU to come INTO THE FULL KNOWLEDGE OF WHO HE IS, from the letter to THE SPIRIT. THE ONE VOICE THEY KNEW WAS JESUS! We are not the exception.

HOW DOES FAITH COME? IT COMES BY HEARING THE LIFE-GIVING WORD OF GOD. Above man's preaching, GOD IS SPEAKING AND PLACES OUR RESPONSE ON OUR HEARTS. Forgive me for being so repetitive, but the roots of deception go all the way back to the Garden of Eden and if you think the deceiver of Nations plans on letting you go without a fight, you're sadly mistaken. But, the WORD you have been instructed to HEAR WILL BE CLEARER NOW ON HOW TO RESPOND TO HIM FOR WHO HE IS, THE KING OF KINGS. Above just quoting scripture to keep your mind sharp, you must learn to SAY WHAT THE SPIRIT GIVES YOU. A WORD you can't see with your natural eyes, BUT THE TRUE WORD OF GOD THAT SPOKE THE WHOLE WORLD INTO EXISTENCE. IF HE GIVES YOU A SCRIPTURE, HIS SPIRIT WILL BE CREDITED WITH THE RESULTS not your ability or the bible version you learned to memorize.

The scriptures let us know we are to keep our minds stayed ON HIM AND HE WILL KEEP US IN PERFECT PEACE. BUT, THE SPIRIT IS SAYING SO MUCH MORE AND WILL TEACH US THAT all the distractions that we see, hear and think about with the cares of the world are designed to keep us from GROWING IN KNOWING HIS VOICE "Just to remind you so you don't start another movement on faith". The best way I can explain it is: FAITH IS A FRUIT OF THE SPIRIT, SO WHERE DOES FAITH COME FROM? We don't even have the ability to HEAR UNLESS THE WORD GIVES IT TO US, for we can do nothing without HIM, Not even breath. Understand, even if THE WORD WHO IS SPIRIT SPEAKS to our spirit man we might say WHAT HE GAVE US without us even knowing what made us say it. THE POWER IN GOD'S WORD GIVES US LOVE, JOY, PEACE, LONGSUFFERING, GENTLENESS, GOODNESS, FAITH, MEEKNESS, AND TEMPERENCE. BUT, HE DOESN'T JUST STOP THERE. THE WORD OF GOD GIVES US HIS MERCY, GRACE AND TRUTH, A SOUND MIND, WISDOM, KNOWLEDGE AND UNDERSTANDING, LIFE, HEALTH AND STRENGTH, HOPE FOR TOMORROW, THE POWER OVER ALL the works of the devil, HUMILITY, FAVOR, FELLOWSHIP WITH HIM AND REST UNTO OUR SOULS, AN INHERITANCE IN HIS ETERNAL KINGDOM WITHIN AND EVERYTHING PERTAINING TO LIFE AND GODLINESS. SO FAITH COMETH BY HEARING AND THE ABILITY TO HEAR COMES FROM THE WORD OF GOD. Ask Noah, Abraham, Moses, any of the old patriarchs and you can read about all the witnesses of the New Testament.

If you can't HEAR AND KNOW THE SPIRIT, THE WORD AND THE TRUTH, you might be on the wrong foundation.

There's a book in the library titled, *"How the Bible Was Made"*. If you aren't afraid, do your own homework and find out who wrote the bible you carry and all the other ones. You might be surprised to find that some of the divided groups you know to be in more obvious error hold the copyright to the one you carry, swear by, pick up and put down at will, and give it honor and praise without giving John 1:1-14 a second thought. Then, after doing the homework, tell me it's the only infallible Word of God. If you are going to be a follower, FOLLOW JESUS AND BE A LIVING TESTIMONY.

People haven't changed much from when JESUS WALKED ON THE EARTH IN THE FORM OF A MAN. There were people who BELIEVED ON HIM, but were afraid to openly CONFESS HIM for fear of the religious folk who were at the top of their game religiously, proclaiming to be masters of the letter, therefore they were not to be disputed. Will a Spirit of fear stop you from saying what THE SPIRIT OF TRUTH AND the Spirit of UNITY AND DELIVERANCE SAYS? Will you now SEEK TO BE EMPOWERED, CORRECTED, COME OUT OF HIDING behind the leaves of a tree by-product (paper) and just be honest before your maker, FOR HE KNOWS EVERYTHING about you any way. The only ones you are able to fool at times are the same ones you play hide and seek with.

WHEN HE IS CREDITED FOR TEACHING YOU AND SENDING YOU, THEN YOU WILL LIVE BY EVERY WORD THAT PROCEEDETH OUT OF THE FATHER'S MOUTH AND, TOGETHER WITH HIM, YOU WILL FEED THE HUNGRY SOULS that are starving from the lack of SPIRITUAL FOOD AND THE FELLOWSHIP IN THE KINGDOM WHERE THE FEAST OF THE LORD IS GOING ON.

Today, there are so many dear souls caught up in leading alone. They are powerless to follow, especially THE WORD OF GOD because HE WILL NEVER LINE UP with the doctrines of men not submitted to anyone in their church where they are "the head" and have the final say on everything. They major in the epistles, jumping over what JESUS SAID, stumbling at THE WORD as recorded in 1st Peter 2:6-8, not understanding that THE LEADING OF THE SPIRIT WILL GIVE them a WAY OUT OF bondage and everyone connected with them.

Our church or HIS CHURCH?

THE Song says, "When THE CHURCH begins to pray, YOU CAN HAVE YOUR OWN WAY." Let's agree that THE SPIRIT OF TRUTH MOVES IN TRUTH. THE CHURCH I'm referring to is none other than THE CHURCH JESUS SAID HE WOULD BUILD. I can't figure out for the life of me how we could have followed tradition for so long and not noticed we've been lied to. But I suppose as long as someone is deceived they can't see that THE TRUTH THAT MAKES US FREE has not been made known to them. That's the reason for this book.

To explain where I'm going, let's go back to the Garden of Eden. We understand Adam's bride was deceived by the deceiver which led to Adam disobeying the WORD OF GOD WHOM he TALKED WITH. Since Satan had such success in deceiving Adam's bride, what would be so difficult in deceiving even JESUS' bride? JESUS' CHURCH WAS ESTABLISHED BY HIM, not man. For, HE SAID UNTO Peter who received REVELATION FROM THE FATHER AS TO "WHO JESUS WAS", that

ON THIS REVELATION HE WOULD BUILD HIS CHURCH AND the gates of hell will not prevail against it. This is what THE WORD OF GOD IN JESUS SAID and it was recorded that HE WOULD GIVE US AUTHORITY OVER all the works of the devil. HE IS THE HEAD, THE FOUNDER AND THE KING APOSTLE. HE REFERS TO THE CHURCH HE'S BUILDING AS HIS BRIDE, EVEN HIS BODY, ONE IN HIM. We would do well to obey the command TO LOVE.

Eph. 5:23 SAYS: "for the husband is the head of the wife, even as "CHRIST IS THE HEAD OF THE BODY". Have you thought about how many new churches people will start, and how many splits on top of that? I know people's intentions are good, but unless we are GOVERNED FROM THE KINGDOM OF HEAVEN BY OUR FATHER'S WORD, we are powerless to stay submitted TO HIS WILL or HIS SPIRIT OF TRUTH here on the earth.

We "MUST BE EMPOWERED BY HIM" TO FOLLOW THE SPIRIT OF TRUTH that even Paul wrote about. We read in Ephesians 1:17 THAT "THE GOD OF OUR LORD JESUS CHRIST, THE FATHER OF GLORY, MAY GIVE YOU THE SPIRIT OF WISDOM AND KNOWLEDGE 'OF HIM'" Found in most Christian BIBLES. In order to not believe every spirit, we MUST COME TO KNOW HIS VOICE, HIS WORD, HIS SPIRIT OF TRUTH, PEACE AND UNITY IH HIM. You can try the spirits. Are they for UNITY IN GOD or that which adds to division?

Hopefully, by now we are getting closer to being built up IN THE SPIRIT OF HUMILITY IN SUBMITTING TO HIM WHOSE PRAYER IS FOR US TO BE ONE! As we BECOME ONE IN HIM, HE CAN BRING US TOGETHER "IN HIM" VOID OF self-seeking, self-promoting, self-righteousness, or any other spirit outside THE REALM OF HIS GOVERNING RULE.

Here's a thought. How can a person stay on the straight and narrow if they have no knowledge OF HIM? Just like we MUST KNOW WHO JESUS IS, we must also know WHO THE CHURCH IS AND SPEAK ACCORDING TO THE TRUTH IN ORDER FOR HIM TO AGREE WITH WHAT WE SAY BECAUSE THE SPIRIT OF TRUTH MOVES IN TRUTH, ACCORDING TO OUR FATHER'S DEFINITION OF TRUTH. Then, we will SEE HIS WILL BEING DONE HERE ON EARTH in a time when we need HIM the most to HEAL our land. Look around you again at a lost world lost in chasing the ups and downs of the financial world. You already know how our prisons are filled to capacity. All the kingdoms of the world have great appeal, so much so, even an offer was made to JESUS. Read or re-read Matthew 4:1-11 in any Christian version. All the kingdoms include all the religious kingdoms outside THE KINGDOM OF OUR FATHER.   Now the big question is this: If whatever decisions we make originate in the spirit realm, what spirit would inspire a person to start their own church, win people to JESUS, and in the next birth persuade them to join something they don't even have any "sound" Biblical basis for? Still, there might be a bible or two out there that might misinterpret or suggest that man's knowledge of scripture or a degree from one of the many different scho of thought somehow qualifies a person to become the head sheep over all the blind! Ask yourself what we have been offered and expected from an enemy that would tempt THE WORD OF GOD IN THE FLESH and even entice men to put HIM to death. Do you think it might be possible that the idea of having their own church and doing all the good works people do can somehow excuse rebellion? The lying spirits think we are too weak to regroup and LET HIM USE US TO MAKE the kingdoms of the world THE KINGDOMS OF OUR GOD!

THE CHURCH JESUS IS BUILDING is made up of dear souls HE GAVE HIS LIFE FOR. That's us! Now that the cat is out the bag, so to speak, THE CALL HAS GONE OUT IN THE SPIRIT and into our cities for those who will make themselves willing to be chosen by HIM WHO SEARCHES our hearts, and KNOWS AND CHOOSES US BY HIS OWN DIVINE, RIGHTEOUS JUDGEMENT. You can search the scriptures to see if, in them, you have eternal life but you have to GO TO HIM TO OBTAIN IT. Otherwise, people simply turn the page and go on in their own self-righteousness. As you continue to read, my prayer for you is that you push past being offended even as you would go through the valley of the shadow of death LOOKING UNTO THE LORD AS YOUR SHEPHERD, AND LET HIM LEAD YOU INTO WHAT HE HAS FOR YOU. Look at following JESUS BEYOND TIME BUT FOLLOW HIM TO BE MADE ONE IN HIM AND IN UNITY WITH ALL THAT IS WITHIN HIM. Can you hear the Spirit that's trying to convince you that you can't have your own preferred church and another head who knows the bible better than anyone under him or her? Until THE LORD BRINGS us together SOVEREIGNLY, let us learn how to walk together in love with our family members. let THE LORD TEACH US HOW TO FORGIVE and respect those closest to us so we will KNOW HOW TO LOVE, FORGIVE, RESPECT, AND WALK IN PEACE AND UNITY AMONG HIS FAMILY MEMBERS WHEN HE BRINGS US TOGETHER.

FROM division in King James TO UNITY IN KING JESUS SPEAKS VOLUMES BEYOND my ability to articulate. Where are THE TRUE GIFTS GOD HAS GIVEN US ALL right here in our City? As much as I would like to think everyone will make the turn and allow THE LORD TO HEAL OUR LAND the spirit of fear in a person's heart can blind them from seeing. WHATEVER OUR FATHER HAS FOR US IS FAR GREATER THEN ANYTHING WE CAN see in the natural world THAT HE MADE AND GAVE TO MAN BEFORE the fall.

NO ONE LEFT BEHIND SHOULD BE OUR MOTTO.

I was in the military and one of the worst places to be when engaging the enemy is caught in between crossfire between both sides. But for the sake of a fellow solder you might be the only one in position to go to his aid. Nowhere in the bible, properly translated and interpreted, is a man-made building called THE CHURCH. How could we adopt the tradition of men in building buildings and call them THE CHURCH? And anyone who starts one could give it a different name to make sure there was a clear difference in theirs from all the rest.

Some people reading this book might feel as though they are in between not just good and evil BUT TRUTH and the lie. IN KNOWING THE LORD IS YOUR SHEPHERD, like David, HE WILL LEAD YOU THROUGH the valley of the shadow of death also. This entire book is designed to make sure we keep the main thing the main thing, as a friend of mine told me. No doubt we will have a clear picture of where we're at, but more importantly, "where we're going".

For us to continue in the traditional way we've been trying to express THE LOVE OF GOD, divided and out of order, we would have to reject THE TRUTH, THE SPIRIT, AND THE WORD WHICH ARE ONE.

THE LORD's order for HIS CHURCH in I Corinthians 12:27-28, "now ye are THE BODY OF CHRIST and members in particular. . ." Not members by joining something. You can join yourself with any group without actually joining it, but in the BODY OF CHRIST You must be BORN INTO HIS FAMILY OR ADOPTED, THERE IS NOTHING TO JOIN.

A few things we want to go over before we come to the end of this book are:
    1. THE LORD'S CHURCH IS FOUNDED ON THE ALMIGHTY WORD OF GOD;
    2. HE'S BUILDING PEOPLE AND BRINGING THEM TOGETHER IN HIS WILL;
    3. THE SPIRIT OF TRUTH WON'T ALLOW ANY OLD THING TO BE BUILT ON JESUS;
    4. Good works are no substitute for obeying and following THE TRUTH, and

5. HIS GOVERNMENTAL ORDER FOR HIS CHURCH IS FOUND IN EPHESIANS 4:11-12. THE LORD'S APOSTOLIC GIFTS would lay down their lives IF NEED BE FOR TRUTH OF GOD'S WORD.

From now on you will view people differently who call the bible, in and of itself, the Word of God no matter which one of thousands. But, deceived, unknowingly walking in division from everyone else and their own walk in confusion lets people know they don't obey their own preferred Word of God. Instead of following tradition where every time there's a disagreement in doctrine or misunderstanding and there's a split, in most cases, another person rises up and becomes the pastor and the head of another church/organization. No scripture.

Every member of THE BODY WAS BORN INTO HIS CHURCH. Every local group no matter the size, from a house group to those who worshiped in caves, in synagogues, on the side of a hill like Reservoir Park in Harrisburg, Pa. wherever they met, they knew the difference between THE CHURCH AND THE PLACE where they worshiped or assembled. This TRUTH THE SPIRIT ORDAINED AND SUPPORTED BY ADDING TO THE CHURCH AT HIS WILL.

If you're still being led by THE TRUTH, you can see that when Paul and others would communicate with each other by letters they were united enough to address THE WHOLE CHURCH IN every city. IN 1ST CORINTHIANS Verse 2 we read, "unto THE CHURCH OF GOD which is at Corinth to them that are sanctified in

Christ JESUS, called to be saints with all that in every place call upon THE NAME OF JESUS CHRIST OUR LORD, both theirs and ours:.. . ." Check your bible version and go back to verse 1 showing how Bro Paul never referred to himself as "THE" APOSTLE PAUL. It reads I, Paul, an Apostle OF JESUS CHRIST BY THE WILL OF GOD and Timothy our brother, unto THE CHURCH OF GOD which is at Corinth, with all the saints which are in all Achaia. Can you see THE CHURCH OF THE LORD JESUS UNITED in your city? Can OUR FATHER use you to stand against the lies of the deceiver?

Revelation 2:1 reads, Unto the angel of the Church "of" Ephesus", but Ephesus never gave birth to the LORD's CHURCH, so it should read THE CHURCH "in" Ephesus.

"It may be a small thing to some but the deceiver would use any little thing he can to confuse and deceive us to "not walk together IN THE SPIRIT OF TRUTH." Little things that would keep people at odds with each other in the scriptures and never understand we will never come together in agreement about the scripture UNTIL WE ARE ONE IN THE WORD. Because when we take our eyes off the one the scripture is meant to point us to we get into error. Again, if you call anything other than GOD THE WORD OF GOD, then that is the only word you know, one you can see and interpret sometimes right and sometimes wrong. Another problem is everyone has their own version, interpretation, translation and not one is perfect or can walk or talk. THE TRUTH IS people can turn it any way they want and make it (their definition of the Word) say just about anything they want it to. I use mostly the rainbow study Bold-letter edition of the bible where every verse is color coded. The King James Version, source of most English American versions, by the way, was never mentioned with THE FATHER, SON AND HOLY GHOST. Revelation of WHO JESUS IS would never allow you to exalt King James "a" Word above KING JESUS "THE" WORD, PERFECT IN ALL HIS WAYS and no lie IN HIM AT ALL!

Now, if we had set in on the very conversations between the men who God used to write these letters, no devil could deceive us as to what they meant but we don't have that privilege and neither did the thousands of translators over thousands of years and there are more interpretations then there are different churches founded by man.

Let me say this on behalf of the bibles. There's enough written Truth, if interpreted and applied correctly, to point the world in the right direction. With one major exception, it must not be void of the support of THE SPIRIT, THE TRUTH and agree with THE ALMIGHTY WORD OF GOD THAT GIVES LIFE TO EVEN THE LETTER. Without THE SPIRIT, the letter alone is dead and subject to anyone's interpretation. It's THE SPIRIT THAT GIVETH LIFE AND THAT MUCH MORE ABUNDANTLY! Instead of all the dead divided churches men boast in, let us together boast in THE LIVING RISEN LIVING SAVIOUR. Finding fellowship with any one open to THE WORD OF GOD outside the buildings and their doctrines.

CHAPTER EIGHT

A divided UNITED STATES.

At last, I can get to one of my favorite chapters to further establish sound biblical instructions with an ear to HEAR FROM THE SPIRIT TO FOLLOW THE LEADING OF THE LORD. How many times have those of us that confess to KNOW THE WORD OF GOD read 2nd Chronicles 7:14. AND it reads as recorded that "THE LORD SAID", "IF MY PEOPLE, WHICH ARE CALLED BY MY NAME, SHALL HUMBLE THEMSELVES, AND PRAY, AND SEEK MY FACE, AND TURN FROM THEIR WICKED WAYS: THEN WILL I HEAR FROM HEAVEN, AND WILL FORGIVE THEIR SIN, AND WILL HEAL THEIR LAND". I BELIEVE THE VERY SAME GOD IS SAYING TO US TODAY (in my own words), DO you think because things look so bad HE IS not able to heal our land? As a people who have cried out to the government, cursed The Person you see as the answer to the sins of the Whole Nation, marched, held all night prayer meetings out of fear. Everything but repent and turn from our wicked ways! Of choosing another only infallible word of god over HIM! Being left to yourself you can't HEAR HIM, or even think that, that's the problem. Now, if I'm off base and you need to set someone straight, don't call me because if you can't HEAR GOD AND KNOW HIM TO HAVE THE ANSWERS TO ALL of life's problems it matters less what I say. And I am not about to argue with you about issues of not only your head but your heart. Listening to some Christian talk shows cursing and accusing people openly by name, even the highest office in the land. Not understanding they're subject to spirits that lie just like anyone out from under THE SHADOW OF THE ALMIGHTY, it makes me wonder what would JESUS SAY? FOR HE WAS AND IS NOT A RESPECTOR of persons AND SPOKE DIRECTLY TO ALL the hypocrisy and sanctimonious self-righteous religionists that thought they knew everything but did not KNOW THE LIVING WORD OF GOD, HIS SPIRIT or have A heart to BELIEVE, EVEN WITH ALL THE MIRACLES ONLY GOD COULD HAVE DONE.

I hear some people trying to convince those listening to them of how good things were years ago. I must have missed those years because as long as I can remember most people in my neighborhood years ago would beg to differ. For those who have been raised in the middle class, all or most of their life things might have looked pretty good. But in the 40's, 50's, even the 60's, a lot of Americans were still riding in the back of the bus. I won't go down the long list of things a freed people were not free to do. Today, I understand our battle is not with flesh and blood, but with an enemy we can't see. Scripture interpreted correctly reads in Ephesians 6:12-17:

"For we wrestle not against flesh and blood, but against principalities, against powers, against the rulers of the darkness of this world, against spiritual wickedness in high places. 13 Wherefore take unto you the whole armor of God "that" ye may be able to withstand in the evil day, and having done all, to stand. 14 Stand therefore, having your lions girt about with truth, and having on the breastplate of righteousness; 15 And your feet shod with the preparation of the gospel of peace; 16 Above all, take the shield of faith, wherewith ye shall be able to quench all the fiery darts of the wicked. 17 And take the helmet of salvation, and the sword of the Spirit, which is the word of God:" (THE RAINBOW STUDY BIBLE).

One day as I was driving, I pulled up behind a car and it had a bumper sticker that read: Don't trust whitey. I thought there are still people in 2013 still blaming the white man for what is orchestrated from the unseen. And, as I was passing him, to my amazement, he was Hispanic. I thought Satan is a trip! It just goes to show that lying spirits don't respect color or religion but he goes about seeking whomsoever he may devour, and will have anyone and everyone blaming someone else for them not having THE RIGHT RELATIONSHIP IN THE PEACE OF GOD THAT SURPASSES ALL HUMAN UNDERSTANDING UNITED WITH THE FAITH OF GOD FOR HIS WILL TO BE DONE HERE ON EARTH AS IT IS IN HEAVEN. THE LOVE OF GOD THAT CASTETH OUT fear IN ORDER FOR THE FAITH OF GOD TO WORK BY THE LOVE OF GOD THAT COVERS A MULITITUDE of sin. Just ask the rich and famous what's missing in their life if they don't have a right relationship with their creator. Ask them are they exempt from problems dealing with worry, health, and the issue of life after death. Let me remind you that there is more to ABUNDANT LIFE than chasing the ups and downs of the financial index. OUR FATHER HAS MADE the playing field level when it comes to obtaining THE REAL PEACE OF GOD. The longer this country or any other country chooses the different spirits behind pin and paper as the only Infallible Word Of God, avoiding GOD, this country like the traditional man-made churches will stay in division and denial, confusion, and void of THE WISDOM OF OUR CREATOR OF THE UNIVERSE to govern the rich, poor and the middle class. Then, we will see THE GLORY OF GOD AS WE "TOGETHER" REACH A LOST WORLD that's waiting for THE CORRECTED SONS OF OUR FATHER TO BE MANIFESTED IN THE SPIRIT OF LOVE, PEACE AND UNITY!

As more and more people who have never had to experience the possibility of losing house, retirement, health benefits, investments and what some call the good life, let's try and understand why would GOD ALLOW the covering to be pulled off the most powerful nation in the world to not know how to fight its greatest enemy: lying spirits that can't be seen with the naked eye. And, allow the whole world to see the fruit of deception in a divided UNITED STATES? As we ALLOW THE SPIRIT OF TRUTH TO ESTABLISH US TOGETHER ON THE RIGHT FOUNDATION OF GOD'S HEALING AND DELIVERING WORD, HE CAN RAISE UP PEOPLE TO openly cry out to HIM FOR the people we are to pray as opposed to cursing them by name to hell as the spirit of the devil gives them utterance as we begin to convey the same message that we all are on the same level playing field where we all must choose to SUBMIT OURSELVES TO THE RULE OF THE WORD OF OUR FATHER. THE DIFFERENCE IN GOD'S WORD and man's words is, WHEN GOD SAYS WHOSOEVER WILL, HE MEANS WHAT HE SAYS. On the other hand, if you've lived for any length of time you already know that all men are subject to lie. There is something I must mention up front. We can't play HIM BECAUSE HE KNOWS JUST WHAT we will think for as long as we live. So, in your searching and listening for GOD'S WORD DIRECTLY TO you, be like Jacob and don't let HIM GO UNTIL HE BLESSES Your soul, even if you might be injured in the process. Read or re-read Gen 32:24-30.

Establish this truth in your heart, that our CREATOR NEVER created anything greater than or as satisfying AS HIMSELF! Take it from someone who KNOWS FIRST HAND BY BEING FILLED WITH HIS HOLY GHOST beyond A TOUCH OR A CALL TO GET OUR ATTENTION. IF WE ARE TO BE UNITED WITH HIM, OUR SPIRIT MAN MUST BE MADE ONE IN HIM! Instead of looking back at what some call "the good old days," let's look UNTO THE LORD WHO INSPIRED our Bro Paul to write Corinthians 2:9 "But as it is written, Eye hath not seen, nor ear heard, neither have entered into the heart of man, the things which GOD HATH PREPARED FOR THEM THAT LOVE HIM". Most messages today are directed to the needs of the natural man so people's eyes are on the things of this world. But, I remember a message that explained WITH GOD YOU CAN HAVE YOUR CAKE AND EAT IT TO.

THERE IS IN ANSWER TO ALL the different problems this nation faces and we find them IN THE ALL-KNOWING-ALL-WISE CREATIVE WORD OF GOD. Example: Do you believe it was the little half-hearted prayers that was taken out of the schools that kept the schools from all the violence that has been taking place in them? Do you think just maybe, THE LORD ALLOWED us to see how we as a whole did not give HIM THE CREDIT FOR KEEPING OUR CHILDREN SAFE? Any time people can give credit to anything other than HIM we end up getting into error. Answer me this: who is supposed to get the GLORY when we read the scriptures and apply them to heart and THE SPIRIT MAKES MANIFEST WHAT WE BELIEVED? Do we give the PRAISE AND GLORY TO the scriptures, the bible, or our ability to know how to make the word of god (a tree by-product) work for us out of knowledge of a private interpretation? Remember the Egyptians being the greatest nation on the earth at one time but ended up worshiping the sun, the moon, snakes, all sorts of things, including man. AND THE LORD HAD TO allow them to be torn away from all the idolatry and degradation they were in. How can a person give THE ALMIGHTY ALL THE HONOR, GLORY AND EVEN RESPECT DUE HIM IF they don't KNOW HIM?

"THE IMPORTANCE OF THE CHURCH OF GOD IN THE UNITED STATES"

Do you see the vast difference in the interpretation of man's churches and JESUS' CHURCH? I hate to admit it, but we all have been deceived in this area. But THE GRACE AND MERCY OF GOD AND THE COMPLETE VICTORY JESUS GOT OVER the enemy REDEEMED US WHO RECEIVE HIM. Unlike the first Adam Who gave up everything, THE LAST ADAM RECOVERED EVERYTHING, A PLACE IN HIS KINGDOM, ETERNAL LIFE, A RIGHT TO THE TREE OF LIFE, and POWER OVER ALL the works of the spirits that lie. As we give up our wills to do anything we want HE CAN EMPOWER US TO BE HUMBLE ENOUGH, TO PERFECT US AS HIS CHURCH, AND the very gates of hell will not be able to prevail against US! Do you

BELIEVE HE HAS THE POWER TO BRING HIS CHURCH TOGETHER USING EVERYONE THAT TRULY UNDERSTANDS HOW MUCH WE NEED ONE ANOTHER FOR HIS BODY TO MOVE AS ONE, HERE ON THE EARTH?

We should be so in touch with each other in the cities, ALL THE CHURCHES EVERYWHERE WOULD HAVE FELLOWSHIP, RELATIONSHIP OR CONNECTION BY THE SPIRIT WITH ALL THE GIFTS JESUS HAS GIVEN, NOT JUST A PASTOR! Listen to THE SPIRIT AS you read what Isaiah wrote in Chapter 53, Verse 6: "All we like sheep have gone astray; we have turned everyone to his own way; and THE LORD HATH LAID ON HIM the iniquities of us all". We, as members of HIS BODY are also likened as to sheep and guess WHO THE PASTOR IS?
JESUS SAID: "I AM THE GOOD SHEPHERD AND KNOW MY SHEEP AND AM KNOWN OF MINE" (John 10:14). When did JESUS' SHEEP become man's sheep?
Or get this, when did the bride take on a bride of her own? Could it be that the world just models what it perceives to be the church run by preacher's gone crazy?

I hope you don't skip over these scripture verses because they are tools left by men who gave up their lives to try and keep THE UNITY OF THE FAITH. These tools must line up with THE SPIRIT OF TRUTH or they will be misused to further fund division not OUR FATHER'S KINGDOM INTO THE HEARTS of people that GOD CAN USE to turn this country OVER TO HIM. Sooner or later, parents will have to be the ones to teach their children that they are a temple, that prayer will be a part of who they are IN RELATIONSHIP WITH GOD, that no devil in hell can stop them from TALKING WITH THEIR HEAVENLY FATHER AND MAJORING ON HEARING AND KNOWING HIS VOICE. HAVING A REAL RELATIONSHIP WITH THE CREATOR NOT ONLY IN SCHOOL BUT EVERYWHERE they go! Read to them about a child named Samuel, the 3rd chapter 1-21. REVELATION OF WHO JESUS IS GIVES US KEYS TO THE KINGDOM FROM WHERE WHATEVER HE SAYS HIS SOVEREIGN WORD IS SO. AND WE WHO BELIEVE WILL SEE THE MANIFESTATION OF WHAT HE MEANT. John 10:14 recorded that JESUS SAID "I AM THE GOOD SHEPHERD, AND KNOW MY SHEEP, AND AM KNOWN OF MINE" (Verse 27). JESUS, GOD'S WORD SAID: "MY SHEEP HEAR MY VOICE, AND I KNOW THEM AND THEY FOLLOW me". The key here again is to HEAR HIS VOICE IN ORDER TO FOLLOW HIM! If you don't understand WHO JESUS IS, THE ONLY TRUE AND LIVING RISEN GOD, then you will not benefit or value WHAT HE SAYS or even have an ear to hear from anyone outside someone else you call the pastor.

When the church, HIS CHURCH, begins to pray (now that we know who we are) HE CAN HAVE HIS OWN WAY. Remember II Chronicles 7:14.
There will come a time when you must make THE DECISION TO HEAR, BELIEVE AND OBEY THE WORD OF THE LORD and not be afraid of hearing and following the wrong spirit. As I stated before, and the reason for the exercise in your Bible, is to let you know who HE IS NOT! FOR HE IS THE WHOLE FACTOR

TO the voice you have been following up until this point. I am not talking about divided misunderstandings in scripture which the Spirit of the deceiver wants us to believe is the only infallible Word of God and not acknowledge OUR FATHER'S WORD OF GOD FOR WHO HE IS, Making a person ineffective IN OBEYING THE WORD OF TRUTH.

The warning also is this: THE PERFECT WORD OF OUR FATHER needs no interpreter WHEN HE SPEAKS DIRECTLY TO SOMEONE. BUT, HE MAY SHOW YOU your heart like HE DID WITH the rich young ruler who thought he would be losing something more important than OBEYING GOD'S WORD. Read or re-read Matthew 19:16-26. I'm reminded of one man who was being tested and asked THE LORD TO help his unbelief! That shows a heart sold out to the fact that WITHIN JESUS WAS THE ANSWER TO WHAT he needed. Those who are TRULY OPEN TO RECEIVE HIS WORD WILL EVEN BE OPEN TO HIS WORD OF CORRECTION.

Those who will not receive correction simply don't understand that HIS WAYS are not our ways and the only way we can be LED BY AND WALK WITH GOD IS to be close enough, long enough to KNOW HIS VOICE IN THE MIDDLE OF a storm. And what I LOVE ABOUT OUR GOD IS: you can be deaf and HEAR HIM THROUGH THE SPIRIT. Do you remember when you first ACCEPTED CHRIST AS YOUR PERSONAL SAVOUR? YOU RESPONDED TO MORE than the Preacher's call to openly show yourself as a BELIEVER ON JESUS THE CHRIST? There was something or should I say SOMEONE, EVEN MINISTERING

SPIRITS, URGING you to respond. You probably don't remember the message preached that day, but you do remember a Spiritual change. Only the Words that line up with THE TRUTH AND MADE ALIVE BY THE SPIRIT ARE ABLE TO FIND A PLACE IN OUR HEARTS.

There must be a clear understanding to everyone NOT TO LET THIS OPPORTUNITY PASS! FOR HIS MERCY AND GRACE COULD BYPASS this generation as to the next steps to take for this country and THE POTENTIAL CHURCH the nation will be influenced by. There have been many prayer groups coming together to deal with different issues, but have there ever been a people separated from the different traditional man-made organizations UNITED without any hidden motives of division outside THE KINGDOM OF OUR FATHER GOVERNED BY HIS WORD TO BRING GLORY TO HIS NAME? For truly the harvest is great today, but the laborers are few. Men's churches have a name given usually by the one who started it and is usually referred to being a building made by the hands of man or a man-made organization. Usually the leader of that "church" is called "the" pastor regardless of whether or not that was the gift God gave or not. In most cases, it's like trying to fit a large square peg into a small round hole. WHAT IS MEANT FOR HIS CHURCH IS FOR HIS CHURCH, and won't work in someone
else's misunderstanding, but it will produce more deception! It's like a fly caught in a spider's web, the more the fly tries to shake it-self lose the more it entangles "it-self". Please stop and think. The problem has been somehow the enemy has kept peoples' eyes off THE SPIRITUAL and on the natural with another version of

91

God's Word. The man-made church usually has their own order for leading people who can't see. In place of THE GIFTS GOD GAVE, every divided group has their own pastor, assistant pastor, associate pastors, youth pastors, home group pastors, prison ministry pastors and aspiring "want to be" pastors and so on.

Do you see why there is so much division and private interpretations about scripture governing man's organized misunderstandings? Some can do part but can't understand other parts, unable to see through the eye of UNITY. I hate to say it again but we will never agree on scripture until we are positioned to make the scriptures lined up with THE WORD OF OUR FATHER' and we find UNITY IN HIM. That my dear brothers and sisters will only happen when we become willing to submit to THE SAME MASTER BUILDER WHOS WORD exceed that of today's equivalent of the scribes and Pharisees and the wise and prudent. We don't have the Pharisees today. But the Spirit is still the same. There's No one gift that can receive all of THE TRUTH FROM HIS WORD WHEN HE GAVE ALL THE GIFTS FOR THE PERFECTING OF THE SAINTS, for the work of the ministry for the edifying of THE BODY OF CHRIST. "Till we all come INTO THE UNITY OF THE FAITH, and of THE KNOWLEDGE OF THE SON OF GOD UNTO A PERFECT MAN, UNTO THE MEASURE OF THE STATURE OF THE FULLNESS OF CHRIST. (Ephesians 4:12, 13).

Apostles and Prophets deal with a lot of things, but one thing they major in and that is HEARING AND OBEYING THE WORD OF GOD. For there is "no other foundation" than THE LORD JESUS CHRIST, THE

SAME WORD THAT WILL JUDGE THE WORLD. Just a few more lines and the pain of this operation will be over. Then, you who are not fearful will receive a WORD OF HEALING so that when you preach deliverance and recovery to others, you will do so from a position of experience not from entertainment or to separate from THE BODY OR THE CHURCH OF THE LORD JESUS THE ALMIGHTY WORD MADE FLESH.

Here is the work of the deceiver who, when in HEAVEN, decided to exalt himself above THE ALMIGHTY. When given the opportunity to deceive people, part of his goal was to influence people to self-exalt themselves. To affect a whole Nation like this one, here's an amazing scripture that lets us know OUR FATHER IS STILL MORE THAN ABLE regardless of how things look, TO HEAL OUR LAND.

Here is the Word of Healing

No matter where you are, no matter who you are, we all must come the same way. The way up is down. I've followed tradition before and was made a pastor in man's words only. So, without understanding GOD'S ORDER OF BUILDING, I tried to follow tradition without the other gifts working together. I tried to break out of the box but people want what they want – a traditional pastor that governs by time, not eternity. So whatever you do don't discredit THE LEADING OF THE LORD and don't let people be the cause of you not being free to be what your HEAVENLY FATHER PURPOSED FOR YOU TO BE. WHO KNOWS HE MIGHT USE YOU GIVE A WORD OF HEALING TO THIS divided UNITED STATES?

Here again is a Word of healing. AS THE LORD BUILDS HIS CHURCH FOR the Nation to turn to as to what SAITH THE LORD? FOR GOD TO CHANGE a People that religiously opposed one another into ONE WOULD BE one of the greatest miracles of this generation. For brother to LOVE brother past race and religion could only be AN ACT OF GOD!

Brother Paul wrote these words to the Philippians (Chap. 2, Verses 1-11)

"If there be therefore any consolation in CHRIST, if any comfort of love, if any fellowship of the Spirit, if any bowels and mercies,2 Fulfill ye my joy, that ye be likeminded, having the same love, being of one accord, of one mind.3 Let nothing be done through strife or vainglory; but in lowliness of mind let each esteem other better than themselves. 4 Look not every man on his own things, but every man also on the things of others. 5 let this mind be in you, which was also in CHRIST JESUS; 6 Who, being in the form of God, thought it not robbery to be equal with God: 7 But made himself of no reputation, and took upon him the form of a servant, and was made in the likeness of men: 8 And being found in fashion as a man he humbled himself, and became obedient unto death, even the death of the cross. 9 Wherefore God also hath highly exalted him, and given him a name which is above every name: 10 That at the name of Jesus every knee should bow, of things in heaven, and things in earth, and things under the earth; 11 And that every tongue should confess that Jesus Christ is Lord, to the glory of God the Father."
(THE RAINBOW STUDY BIBLE)

AS THE CHURCH OF THE LORD JESUS CHRIST BECOMES UNITED IN JESUS

There would be no doubt who to go to as a nation for answers to problems even on a worldwide scale. Don't you think it strange to even think of THE CHURCH OF THE LORD JESUS BEING ANYTHING OTHER THAN UNITED? To REALLY THINK about it, it's so elementary to think GOD HAS TO CORRECT US ON SUCH A BASIC FOUNDATIONAL TRUTH? Especially to a people that have degrees and have mastered "the only infallible word of God." I don't know about anyone else but, by now, if you don't know anything else, you SHOULD KNOW WHO THE NAME OF JESUS BELONGS TO! AND THE ALMIGHTY WORD OF OUR FATHER IS "not" anywhere close to what we thought it was because if anyone's foundation is anything other than THE ALMIGHTY CREATIVE LIVING WORD OF OUR HEAVENLY FATHER THEN THE FOUNDATIONAL TRUTHS OF GOD ARE OUT OF BOUNDS OUTSIDE THE KINGDOM GOVERNED BY HIS SOVEREIGN WORD.

Even though we've read about the first Adam and his help meet being expelled from their covering, which was written for our learning
ABOUT HIM, we are still subject to deception from unseen demonic forces. And, on top of that, using knowledge of good "and" evil as a lure hinders people that GOD LOVES from HEARING, SEEING, "AND" KNOWING THE TRUTH THAT LEADETH INTO ALL TRUTH FOUND IN THE ONLY TRUE WORD OF OUR

MAKER WHO IS ALSO OUR ETERNAL
FOUNDATION WHICH IS THE WORD OF GOD.

If this is your first time understanding that your Bible is a
tool; a treasure chest with information that people lived
through to save you from making some of the same foolish
mistakes they did and points you to THE RIGHT ROAD,
HEADING YOU IN THE RIGHT DIRECTION as long as
you don't try and use it for anything other than the purpose
for which it is intended for? As soon as a spirit tempts you
to use "it" to win THE LORD'S SHEEP into something
unknown or unbiblical or governed by man, check out the
price tag associated to it! How long has it been that people
have been in bondage by acknowledging King James and
not KNOWING KING JESUS? How long will it be
before those you know will be SET FREE BY THE
TRUTH or HEAR, KNOW, LOVE AND OBEY THE
LIVING WORD OF GOD WHO SPEAKS TO HIM OR
HER THAT HAS AN EAR TO HEAR HIM TO KNOW
HOW TO FOLLOW HIM? Will you be the one to tell
them WHO JESUS IS? OR, will you leave them at the
mercy of others who don't know the difference between
pen and paper and SPIRIT AND TRUTH? Make a mental
note that the letter without THE SPIRIT IS dead! BUT
THE SPIRIT MAKETH ALIVE.

If you are in fear of what people will say if you tell others
about JESUS, the best thing to do is spend more time IN
HIS PRESENCE OR in seeking HIM TO HAVE
MERICY. Your testimony of HIM WHEN you come TO
PERSONALLY KNOW HIM is far better than having all
the accolades a person can get from learning Hebrew,
Greek, Latin and Aramaic. The more time you spend IN

LOVE WITH HIS WORD, THE MORE THE WORD WILL REVEAL HIS LOVE TO YOU TO SHARE with those who are open and ready to RECEIVE HIM. We are spiritual beings in a body. When our spirits are not connected to OUR SOURCE we're lost, and being lost means we don't know the way. BUT BEING RECONNECTED BACK TO OUR LIFE SOURCE, OUR CREATOR AND HEAVENLY FATHER, WE ARE GIVEN ACCESS INTO HIS KINGDOM IN A WHOLE OTHER REALM. WHEREVER THE WORD OF GOD IS, BEHOLD THE KINGDOM IS AT HAND, IN YOUR HOME OR ON YOUR JOB. IN HIS KINGDOM IS WHERE THERE IS EVERYTHING ETERNAL. One writer noted, "we're seated WITH HIM IN HEAVENLY PLACES." WHEN WE HAVE BEEN GIVEN ETERNAL LIFE IN AN EXPERIENTIAL way, the problems of this world are only a temporary distraction designed to take your mind off HIM WHO KEEPS YOU IN PERFECT PEACE. When you KNOW YOU ARE KEPT BY THE ALMIGHTY WORD OF GOD everything, and I mean everything, pales in THE LIGHT OF HIM WHO SAID LET THERE BE LIGHT AND THERE WAS LIGHT.

It was also written that, we are in the world but not of "it." Note: having the wrong earthly interpretation of scripture leaves people's mindsets on the things that feed the part of man that seeks knowledge (Head knowledge). If we will but RECEIVE THE SPIRIT OF HIM WHO SPOKE TO the original writers of scripture. we too, like them, will KNOW HIM AND RECEIVE IN OUR SPIRITS "JOY UNSPEAKABLE" AND "FULL OF GLORY!" And, BEING MADE LIVING EPISTLES, HE WILL SPEAK

VOLUMES IN AND THROUGH US TO the world that doesn't KNOW GOD OR HIS WORD. As your earthly knowledge begins to fade in THE LIGHT OF THE KNOWLEDGE OF THE CREATOR OF THE UNIVERSE ("BY HIS WORD"), you will find yourself making scripture line up with what HE MEANT. You will also see how the scriptures are not broken because you have SPIRITUAL EYES AND THE AUTHOR WITHIN "you" WHO KNOWS ALL ABOUT YOU, IS LEADING AND GUIDING, TEACHING AND CORRECTING YOU AS MATURE SONS and AS YOU ARE SUBMITTED TO HIS LOVING WORD WHOM WE LEARN TO LOVE. Even when HE shows us HIS LOVING WORD OF CORRECTION WHICH DELIVERS US FROM MAKING THE SAME MISTAKES AND HAVING TO GO THROUGH agony of defeat when we don't KNOW THE WORD OF GOD THAT SHOWS US THE pitfalls before we venture off and go astray. HE knows all things while we, on the other hand, altogether know nothing!!!

CHAPTER NINE

RECEIVE JESUS, GIVE yourself TO JESUS, EAT, SLEEP, PREACH JESUS IN SEASON AND OUT. LIVE BY EVERY WORD THAT PROCEEDETH FROM OUR FATHER.

We pray this book will be a wakeup call for not only THE CHURCH TO COME INTO UNITY IN JESUS, BUT FOR THE NATION TO BE UNITED IN GOD WHOM WE TRUST. Because you did not recognize His voice or, just rejected the Truth through the Spirit, to acknowledge "JESUS as the Father or infallible Word." How many times have you reasoned within yourself that division was wrong? Where did you go to get an answer to this dilemma? You know, the only source you've been taught to go to, is your version of the Word of God. But, apparently, you remained powerless to do anything but go with the flow. Or, close your ears from hearing the Truth, as the Spirit was speaking while you were reading. (1 Corinthians 1:9-31 and 2:1-16). Now, if you have the strength, please read on with the mindset that you want to hear what the Spirit is saying. For, the Truth and the power to deliver us comes from Him.

We should think again if we believe God wants us to be one as JESUS prayed and used Brother Paul to write about division by exalting mere men over another. If we could be one on our own, apart from Him, we would have done so by now. But, there is no way we can be one except in Him. If it was not so, HE would have told us through at least one of the authors of 66 books. For anyone TRULY SEEKING TO KNOW THE VOICE OF THE LORD,

THERE'S a scripture you need to allow THE SPIRIT TO WRITE ON YOUR HEART. Read or re-read Isaiah 64:4: "For since the beginning of the world men have not heard, nor perceived by the ear, neither hath the eye seen, O God, beside thee, what he hath prepared for him that will wait for him." (Wait ON THE LORD AND AGAIN I SAY WAIT).

In our waiting ON THE LORD, THINK HOW LONG HE HAS BEEN WAITING ON US TO SUBMIT TO HIS PRAYER FOR US TO BE ONE? HE, WHO CANNOT lie, would not tell us and pray for us to be one if it was not possible. If not this generation, then maybe the next or the next. EVERYTHING JESUS SAID WAS PROFOUND, BUT HE ALSO SAID: "WILL HE FIND FAITH ON THE EARTH WHEN HE RETURNS"? We have commented on the faith of some or the lack of faith while reading our Bibles from a position of seeing the whole picture. And, in some cases could not understand how they could be so foolish as to not believe GOD for their DELIVERANCE OR HIS ABILITY TO MAKE A WAY OUT OF NO way. Well, it's our turn to put up or shut up. IS THERE ANYTHING TOO HARD FOR GOD? Then, let's do what we need to do in preparing our families to RECEIVE HIM. AND, HE WILL PREPARE OTHERS TO RECEIVE you HAVING THE WORD OF THE LORD IN your mouth.

Before I close, THE SPIRIT OF WISDOM AND COMPASSION WOULD HAVE us know, there are many, many, many people locked into having their livelihood compromised in letting GOD'S PEOPLE GO and be totally dependent on THE LEADING OF THE LORD BY HIS WORD that they can't see! But in the light of all this,

101

a heart turned towards HIM IN TRUTH IS ALL HE NEEDS TO EXALT the one who will TRULY, TRULY HUMBLE themselves UNTO HIM FOR HIS WILL TO BE DONE HERE ON EARTH AS IT IS IN HEAVEN. WHAT A TESTIMONY FOR those of you WHO WILL GIVE JESUS HIS CHURCH BACK.

One more thing: Music is not the substance that will hold THE CHURCH OF THE LORD JESUS TOGETHER; BUT HIS WORD, WHICH IS SPIRIT AND TRUTH, so the spirit of pride doesn't deceive us like Lucifer. The real good news is, we now know to be open to HEARING HIS WORD FIRST HAND so we can receive the kind of FAITH that cometh by HEARING GOD! In reading this book, we all are challenged to seek HIM from cover to cover. Those of us, who are willing and able to HEAR HIM, will find fellowship IN HIM. Wherever we may be, if there are two or three gathered together, "HE, JESUS," would be in our midst. How good and pleasant it is for brethren to dwell together IN THE SPIRIT OF UNITY. The only ones in THE KINGDOM OF HEAVEN, restored back to man are those given access by THE WORD OF GOD IN THE PERSON OF JESUS THE WORD MADE FLESH.
If you are waiting to die and then hope your good works are enough to get you into THE KINGDOM OF HEAVEN, you are wasting a lot of time. For THE KINGDOM OF OUR FATHER WAS RESTORED BACK to us who BELIEVE BY JESUS' FINISHED WORK. JESUS said, "behold the Kingdom of Heaven is at hand". But, no ungodly division or flesh on parade can bypass JESUS. Do this: re-read how often THE WORD OF OUR FATHER, THROUGH JESUS, repeatedly over

and over and over explained to everyone that HE WAS THE WAY, in every way, the only way. When the self-exalted (Who was limited to their understanding of what they could see challenged HIM with Moses' writings of the law. HE explained how Moses' writings pointed to HIM! But being blind, deaf and dumb (Spiritually) they could not comprehend anyone superseding the law they prided themselves in keeping to the letter. Did you read the 3rd Chapter of 1st Corinthians? We will love the Scriptures even more, "whichever version" IN KNOWING THE ORIGINAL AUTHOR'S VOICE. Only then can its true purpose be applied. JESUS, the Word of God, said the scriptures cannot be broken for everyone's own personal use! (In my own Words).

If you don't believe you must HEAR HIM FOR YOURSELF and only receive what's in writing, here is a note to you: OUR FATHER LOVED US SO MUCH, HE SENT HIS OWN WORD IN THE FORM OF A MAN TO CORRECT, and HEAL AND DELIVER US (That's love. The purpose of this book is to show you HE STILL LOVES US and EVEN IF HE CORRECTS US BY HIS WORD, ITS HIS WORD! My writings just give you a heads up that THE KINGDOM HE OFFERS is void of division. So, in reading anything, read with the mindset of UNITY IN KING JESUS. Then, we won't let another spirit deceive us in division in King James or any other version.

SO THERE IS NO ONE WITHOUT UNDERSTANDING OR LEFT BEHIND.

Consider this thought: Scriptures interpreted correctly let us know that HIS NAME ALONE IS ABOVE every name. And, there is nothing higher than HIS NAME BUT HIS WORD. Now, if your definition of the only infallible Word of God is your bible (whichever version), then you've placed your bible above THE NAME OF JESUS. JESUS IS THE NAME GIVEN TO THE WORD OF GOD! Reread Phil 2:5-11 and do this. Turn to your concordance, if you have one, and check out all the scriptures under "Word". This time, as you read, change your definition of the word of god FROM pen and paper to SPIRIT AND TRUTH. FROM King James TO KING JESUS. FROM a Word that is subject to change with the stroke of a pen to THE ETERNAL ALMIGHTY WORD THAT CHANGES NOT!

Now, it doesn't matter what version you have. What matters is that you know the author's Author. Then, you can hear what HE, THE SPIRIT, IS SAYING TO you or anyone else that has an ear to HEAR HIM. Then, THE FAITH OF GOD, THE LOVE OF GOD, THE PEACE OF GOD, WISDOM, KNOWLEDGE AND THE UNDERSTANDING OF GOD WILL COME.

I must remind you of this so you don't let the spirit that comes to steal, kill, and destroy deceive you into believing you are doing just fine in apprehending the promises OF GOD without having a hunger and thirst for THE PROMISE GIVER. Remember this: that which IS SPIRIT IS SPIRIT and IN THE KINGDOM OF GOD nothing has a price tag attached to it. EVERYTHING IS ETERNAL LIFE LIKE LOVE, JOY, and PEACE IN THE HOLY GHOST. But, the promises that most people seek after

have a price tag attached to them. Even what most call the
Word of God. Anything men can put his hands on goes up
for sale. And, these are the things people chase after but,
the best things in life are free and build the Spirit man.
Our place of worship is a house of prayer for all people
where we assemble or congregate united on one accord in
THE SPIRIT OF LOVE, AS GOD'S FAMILY. THE
CHURCH OF THE LORD JESUS CHRIST, THE TRUE
AND LIVING, RISEN, ETERNAL WORD OF GOD
MADE FLESH SAID HE WOULD BUILD. After being
BORN OUT OF HIS SIDE, REDEEMED, CORRECTED,
TAUGHT AND KEPT BY HIM WHO GAVE HIS LIFE
on a cross for the sins of everyone who will BELIEVE. It's
a place where HE can raise up a people that will reflect
HIS BODY on the earth, a place where all the parts of HIS
BODY are in operation. Whatever your gift, it's valued
and as important as all the others IN GOD'S HANDS;
powerful, powerful tools to be used to point others to HIM.
In GOD'S Governmental order for building HIS CHURCH
HE GAVE GIFTS unto men. All the gifts will point
people to HIM, not them. Our eternal foundation is none
other than THE ALMIGHTY LIFE-GIVING,
UNCHANGEABLE, ONLY TRUE INFALLIBLE WORD
OF GOD WHO IS GOD BUT WAS MADE FLESH.
THAT'S WHO JESUS IS. John 1:1-14.

We believe the different bible versions interpreted
correctly are a powerful tool to be used to point people to
the original Author who not only spoke in times past but
also to anyone who now has an ear to HEAR HIM.

Note: There are some bibles so far off base it would be a
waste of time to try and make sense of them since every

different version is the result of the Spirit that inspired the different groups to make their own different versions according to their belief. Everyone just a little different, but just enough to own copyrights. When anyone says the Bible is the only infallible word of GOD, my question and yours must be which one? Which one spoke this world into existence?

All the major divided Religious groups have their own version.
All the Satanist groups have their different versions.
All the different devil worshippers have their own.
Hitler had his own bible.
All the different cults have their own Bibles.
Many in the world swear by one or the other.
We even have some groups' versions with no knowledge of the Spirit of the copyright holder or their purpose for yet another version to promote their organizations' beliefs or to cash in on the sale of a best seller?
God only knows and the rest of us can only guess. What's so preposterous is some people are so gullible that they own and swear by a version used by the group they know to be in error, but never check who holds all rights.

My point is, don't get confused with another version or your own interpretation of scriptures with THE WORD, THE SPIRIT, THE TRUTH, THE AUTHOR AND FINISHER OF OUR FAITH, THE SOURCE OF LIFE. So,
> Let THE WORD OF GOD BE GOD;
> Let the Bible be the Bible;
> Let the Scripture be interpreted correctly FROM
THE SOURCE;

Let the Church be the Church, and
    Let the house of prayer for all people be just that.

Except the LORD build the church, they that labor, labor in vain.

When people reject THE TRUTH or THE WORD OF CORRECTION, even before they open their mouths, their hearts are an open book before GOD. Could it be HE had rejected them before they rejected HIM? So until their hearts are right before HIM, you might hear just about anything out of their mouths.
So don't take it personally, our assignment is to keep believing and praying IN THE SPIRIT for everyone.

Even as husbands and wives are being made one to reflect JESUS AND HIS BRIDE THE CHURCH, HIS CHURCH, HE IS DEALING with both hearts who have independently been self-centered, self-willed, self-sufficient and self-seeking. So, we can't point the finger at one another, but learn to point each other to HIM WHO HAS ALL POWER IN HIS HANDS to change any and all problems we may face. Keeping in mind who the author of all confusion is where misunderstandings, deception, lies, anger, unforgiveness, bitterness, hatred, envy and strife come from. To him or her that has an ear to hear, especially the preachers and teachers of today's traditional, but organized religious man-made divided groups. Re-read 1 Corinthians 1 again, but this time inquire of the SPIRIT OF UNITY TO OPEN UP your understanding as to what "HE MEANT," concerning "HIS CHURCH!" Not someone else's church, where they are the pastor and final authority to "their church". PLEASE UNDERSTAND:

GOD IS A JEALOUS GOD AND HIS CHURCH/BRIDE IS JOINED TO HIM, not another.

BEHOLD! THE KINGDOM OF HEAVEN IS AT HAND And THE CHURCH IN HARRISBURG, Pa and your city is being called into UNITY ("IN HIM")if you can HEAR WHAT THE SPIRIT IS SAYING, above every other voice of confusion and misunderstanding along with the many distractions that come to keep people from doing their first works over again. In most cases, the called that just went, (not chosen, corrected, empowered, taught and sent).

Believe it or not, there is A CHURCH OF THE LORD JESUS CHRIST IN Harrisburg, Pa and I'm not referring to any man-made unscriptural organization legalized, but not Authorized.

Let me get right to the point because most people have read right over Paul's writing dealing with division IN THE LORD'S CHURCH, in Corinth. So, to THE LORD'S CHURCH IN Harrisburg, Pa, THE LORD IS BUILDING HIS CHURCH and those that don't KNOW HIS VOICE are building theirs, not only using JESUS NAME, but the testimonies of men who had a real experience with THE WORD OF GOD HIMSELF IN the Old Testament and the New.

JESUS' CHURCH IS BORN OUT OF HIS SIDE, like the first Adam. BUT, HIM BEING THE LAST ADAM, THE WORD OF GOD MADE FLESH COULD NOT FAIL. BUT DEFEATED, the deceiver who gave Eve another version of God's word defeated him BY THE ONLY

TRUE LIFE-GIVING WORD HIMSELF. The LORD'S church is born out of his side, being the last Adam.

Man offers KING JESUS, but gives them a steady diet of King James. After having them break all ties with any other church (unknowingly even the one they were just born into) to be submitted to this new religious bondage of division people get into by joining it opposed to all the others. Then, in most cases they're kept in religious bondage by walls of paper or the letter without THE SPIRIT OF TRUTH THAT SETS PEOPLE FREE TO BE ALL HE CREATED US TO BE.

JESUS OFFERS HIS KINGDOM, RULED BY HIS SOVEREIGN WORD, not misunderstanding and misinterpretations. Man offers their interpretation or the interpretation of someone else. What's wrong with division outside THE SPIRIT OF UNITY is that people are deceived when they don't know they are deceived.

BUT THE SPIRIT OF TRUTH DELIVERS AND LEADS INTO ALL TRUTH FOUND IN HIMSELF, and everyone IN HIM IS IN UNITY WITH ALL THAT IS IN HIM!

In order to become A SON that all creation is waiting for is through correction. Otherwise, you are not a SON, but another name used in most Christian Bibles.

The reason people within these paper walls of division haven't been corrected is, they don't know HIS VOICE OR HIS WORD. Any Word outside their division is viewed as opposition. Even a Word from the Spirit must line up with the perpetrating pastor's interpretations of his preferred bible version. In most cases, GODS WORD would be like trying to put new wine into an old wineskin. The rigid thing would burst, so nothing comes in that's unapproved and would cause division within division.

Way too often, people acknowledge the call to all the world. But, before they learn to KNOW THE VOICE OF JESUS TO FOLLOW HIM they are whisked off to join something that increases the number of members joined to whatever they've joined themselves to that look good according to the numbers.

But, THE TRUTH that opposes organized religious order is when those who have been CALLED, CHOSEN, CORRECTED, ANOINTED, MADE RIGHTEOUS, TAUGHT OF THE LORD, KNOW HIS VOICE, LOVE HIM TO OBEY HIM and not another, ACKNOWLEDGING HIM ALL WAYS IN THE SPIRIT OF HUMILITY, GIVEN A GIFT THAT'S UNITED WITH ALL THE OTHER GIFTS, COMPLETELY SATISFIED AND THANKFUL. Being BORN INTO HIS GLORIOUS ROYAL FAMILY there's nothing to join. Even though you can join yourself to a group AS THE LORD LEADS YOU. AND THE WAY HE BEST LEADS IS BY HIS WORD. WHO IS THE HEAD OF HIS CHURCH? I hope this is sinking in" for HE IS THE ONLY HEAD OF THE CHURCH HE GAVE HIS LIFE FOR. And, IN HIM THERE IS NO division, promoting of self, jealousy, envy or strife. But all are submitted or learning to submit to THE TRUTH FIRST AND TO ONE ANOTHER IN THE SPIRIT OF HIS LOVE, RIGHTEOUSNESS AND HUMILITY, SUBJECT TO CORRECTION AS SONS.

Allowing all the gifts to operate with AUTHORITY
FROM THE KING, THERE'S ROOM for all the gifts to
find their place and room to be made for others. We pray
you truly understand that the scriptures "must" line up with
HIM! Not HIM lining up with everyone's
misunderstandings of Who He is Or the difference
between King James and King JESUS.

We have been BLESSED BEYOND MEASURE TO
KNOW THE LOVE OF GOD IN WHO HE IS. For if we
would have been born during any other time in history, we
might not have the vantage point we have, looking at past
history in the scriptures. We're able to see GOD
BRINGING MAN BACK TO HIMSELF, WITH
NOTHING done apart from HIS WORD, according to
scripture interpreted correctly. All who have and those
who will RECEIVE HIS WORD ARE CHANGED BY
HIS WORD, WHICH IS SPIRIT AND TRUTH.
WHATEVER HE PROCLAIMS BY HIS WORD HIS
SPIRIT WILL PERFORM WHAT HIS WILL IS
REGARDING ANY SITUATION.

JESUS IS THE NAME GIVEN TO THE ONLY TRUE
AND LIVING WORD OF OUR FATHER. Amen.

If we go back and TRULY SEEK THE KING, HIS
KINGDOM, AND "HIS" RIGHTEOUSNESS, HE GIVES
US WHATEVER WE NEED, BY HIS SPIRIT.

Then, we go into even the letter with THE WORD OF
THE AUTHOR that everyone else's version must line up

with. Or, they're ever searching the scriptures for some short cut to ETERNAL LIFE.

If a person is deceived in religion, they're on the road to exalt self, (through knowledge), which is the goal of the followers of the deceiver. An impossible feat, (by Satan) who would still like to exalt himself above THE ALMIGHTY. This is "NOT" the fruit of those who "KNOW" the difference between King James and KING JESUS.

THE END_____

Addendum

Additional Thoughts UN-EDITED ~mr

From before time, we see the unity in the Father, His Word and His Spirit. Written revelation explained that in the beginning God made the heavens and the earth and the earth was without form and void and the Spirit moved. Now, this is just my belief: even before God speaks, the Spirit knows God's thoughts and moves to give life when HE speaks.

We can know God by His Spirit Who has blessed us even before HE appears or speaks in ways we understand. The one thing to note is this: being in God's presence. How humble and honest we can be. Fall down on our face and ask Him for mercy. Then, after knowing and learning of Him, we realize how good it is to love Him because of the supernatural agape way HE loves us. If only we would stay in His Love, be established in Him, the proof of our love would be to obey Him.

Listen to what JESUS, the Word of God, said to the woman at the well: "woman, believe Me, and the hour cometh when ye shall neither in this mountain nor yet at Jerusalem, worship the Father. . . Read or re-read John Chapter 4 Verses 22-23 in your preferred version and give the glory to God for opening up your understanding to the scripture.

If the Father is seeking those who will worship Him in Spirit and in Truth, then when HE comes unto you, HE probably will come with His Word. If God would appear and say unto you, "ask what I shall give thee?" What would be your response? The truth is, we don't really know. I would like to think we would ask for wisdom and knowledge like Solomon.

Because of the division and confusion today about the Word of God, the best way I can explain what I've received from the Spirit of Truth is a clear distinction between the Spiritual versus the natural:

1.   Beginning with the Word of God which is God Who speaks.
        a. Then men's natural words without the Spirit, the Truth,
            b. and the Life and all that HE is in one.

2.   The Kingdom of God restored back to us by JESUS.
        a. all the Kingdoms of the world including the religious kingdoms are a result of what spirit offered them the false glory and financial opportunity with them.

3.   The church JESUS is building. The one HE died and rose for.
        a. then somewhere, men of a natural mindset received from another spirit. That man can build his own church with his own hands.

4.   The buildings are called the house of prayer for all people whose house is covered by the Spirit of Truth Who intercedes for us as we learn to come together and get on one accord.

a. man's building called the church takes people's focus away from the Truth as to who they really are.

A better example says the Spirit is this. Draw a line down the center of a piece of paper and you can plainly see. We've been majoring in the minor where there's only division.

THE things of the Spirit - side a
THE things of this world – side b

THE things of the Spirit - side a	THE things of this world – side b
1. THE Word of God	1. Words without life
2. THE Spirit of Truth	2. Deceiving Spirit
3. THE Kingdom of God	3. Men's organizations
4. THE church	4. Man-made buildings
5. THE Spirit of unity	5. Spirits that cause division
6. THE gifts given by God	6. THE pastor/assistant pastor's
7. Love, peace and patience	7. Disobedience, fear, ignorance
8. THE baptism of the Holy Ghost	8. Every other baptism
9. THE good shepherd	9. Man as the pastor alone
10. Apostles and prophets	10. Bishops and pastors

Nothing on side b is to be exalted above side a. We must walk in the Spirit and speak the things that are in line with the Truth in His order.

In writing about the Holy Spirit, you must inquire of Him because HE doesn't just go around boasting in Himself. But what you can appreciate about God is what we must learn. If we're to be one with Him and that is to promote each other like the Father promotes the Son, the Son promotes the Holy Ghost, the Holy Ghost promotes the Son, and the Son promotes the Father. The Father is glorified. His glory covers the whole earth. The Father glorifies JESUS, the Word made flesh. We hear and obey His Voice and HE shares His glory with us through His Holy Spirit. Now the time has come for us together to give Him glory, praise and honor for bringing us into unity in His Kingdom of love, joy, peace, righteousness, mercy and patience, power, humility, wisdom, knowledge and understanding. Everything written about Him that is true is of His Spirit, but anything misinterpreted is not or has hidden motives to deceive by other spirits.

You know JESUS, Who is LORD. HE said, "If you love me, keep my commandments. And I will give you another comforter that HE may abide with you forever, even the Spirit of Truth; Whom the world cannot receive because they seeth Him not, neither knoweth Him: but ye know Him, for HE dwelleth with you, and shall be in you. . . (John14:15-26) King James Version lined up with King JESUS.

Here again, what the Spirit is saying unto the church in the same context and for the single purpose of uniting us in Him, Who liveth.
Read or re-read John 15:17-27 and John 16:1-15.

Can you stand to read just a few more verses? If you've found fellowship in the Spirit Who inspired the men who first wrote what became a part of them, fellowship with the same Spirit gives you better understanding of what they meant even if any part of the original quotes were mistranslated. It's the Spirit that knows the mind of the Father and brings us into unity with Him and them and each other through love. For the Truth, instead of analyzing the writings of old out of a spirit of division, let's come together in unity and obey the things we plainly know to be true, only. HE can make all things plain to us because we've learned to love His Word of correction. I John 5:1-21.

Look for a moment if you will at how we could attack hunger in America, even Africa and the world when we obey the call to unity. How much more effective would our witness be to the lost? How all the assemblies would be edified hearing from the apostles, prophets, evangelists, pastors and teachers. Remember, for the perfecting of the saints, for the work of the ministry, for the edifying of the Body of Christ till we all come in the unity of the faith, and of the knowledge of the Son of God unto a perfect man, unto the measure of the stature of the fullness of Christ: all in unity having one LORD, one faith, one baptism, etc., etc.

What knowledge we could receive from the all-knowing Spirit of God concerning the high crime rates in our cities, in the schools, in the homes. Divorce, homosexuality, crooked leadership in the government and in the pulpit.

We'll see God answering our prayers when we come together in our houses of prayer for all people knowing His Will and standing in Truth and obedience in unity.

I remember when I was in school there were many of us who could not seem to comprehend and no one ever slowed down to make sure we were keeping up. That lesson speaks to us today as believers. No matter how thoroughly we sometimes think everyone understands, there is still the possibility someone may have read the words but had their mind on other things or, the spirits assigned to them may have distracted them from concentrating and seeking the Spirit of God to make his Word alive in them.

One of the hardest things to do is convince a believer to believe something other than what they believe. Because they confess to believers. Believe it or not, even in "what" or who the WORD of GOD is." HE is GOD. HE gives life; HE is true and perfect in every way. HE is alive, HE's the Holy Spirit, HE's one with the Father, and HE has all power in His hands. HE gives us access into the eternal Kingdom restored back to us by His victory over death, Hell, and the grave. HE was given a name above every name. HE was made flesh. Everything HE says comes to be according to his will. Before HE made man to speak, while HE walked on the earth and now that HE lives within us. The whole Kingdom within us is governed by HIS Word.

Who else can have the privilege of being dead and still be alive unto Him. Still able to enjoy family, friends and see the wonderful things the LORD is doing as we are Fighting the good fight of faith and Going through whatever we have to go through.

Preach with demonstration of the Spirit. Preach the Word with power. Preaching the Word and preaching JESUS means the same thing. Just let people know Who JESUS is. Use the bible I pray but make sure you are connected to teachers who are taught by the Spirit, to line the scriptures up with the Truth. And not to make people believe everything you say is the Truth because it's in the bible or by you calling "it" the Word of God. No man can make Him say anything that is not right and true. 66 books alone can't explain or contain Him (John 21:25).

Look at it this way. If the Kingdom of God is within you and his Kingdom is governed by his Word, what would make you think only a few should be led by his voice? And, have rule over all the other Sons of God? By the time you finish this book, you should understand who you are and that the Word of God dwelleth within you. For you are priests and kings, the body of Christ, his bride. One with Him. Him Who? Who is JESUS? Is there a scripture for all those many versions being the almighty Word of God? Where? Who made it?

Is everyone clear and on one accord saying the same thing? Let this be our goal in the Spirit of unity. I've been asked time and time again, how can you know his voice or the Word of God? Well, our forerunners all recorded how the Word of God comes to us. How else could we find Him? Even the ability to hear comes; then faith comes. Along with all the fruit of his Spirit, love, joy, peace, longsuffering, gentleness, (note) faith, meekness, temperance and most Christian bibles read "against such there is no law". No man-made divided organization can box Him in. The unity in his Holy Spirit makes us one in Him, Humbling us in knowing Him Who first knew us. The more we yield ourselves to His loving Word that corrects us, the more we give up our life for His life that's much more abundant. There are other ways you can know His voice, but still it's by His Word directly to you will be unlike anything else you will ever come to know.

This book was given to expose the damage done by being deceived by the Spirit of division in the letter. But the Spirit of unity in Christ makes us one in Him Who paid the extreme price for our redemption with His own blood, then back to unbroken fellowship with our Father, amen.

This book is "not" for the weak, earthly minded, unbelieving, easily offended religious hypocrite who would reject the Truth even in this generation as they did when JESUS, the name given to the almighty Word of God made flesh. Using your preferred translation of scripture, read the Book of John again with a new understanding about the Word of God Who makes us one.

In all their searching for eternal life they think they have enough scriptural knowledge of what has been written already. May God's blessing be upon you and keep you as you go through some of the most challenging reading you have ever faced.

To anyone who can hear what the Spirit is saying, may HE also give you eyes to see. May you have a heart towards Him and the mind of Christ with a love for the almighty Word of our Father, in the person of JESUS (the name translated) the name given to His own.

HE is the "Infallible Word" made flesh. If you have another vision, you're in error, and your foundation is rooted in deception. Therefore, all your good works are done apart from the Spirit of love WHO gives righteousness, humility, correction, truth and unity. Wherein they too can know Him Who called them, chose them, taught them and ordained them, anointed them, and sanctified them, baptized them in Himself, then sent them.

In place of being a slave to the natural earthly knowledge of man who by the spirit of division would have you deceived into believing that being double-minded is correct interpretation of scripture. One faith, one baptism, one in Him Who is true, means you must seek the Almighty, Who empowers us to submit ourselves to Him alone. It is He Who has the wisdom, power and authority in His Word. By His Spirit He does the impossible and makes humble Sons, kings and priests heirs of His glorious Kingdom which we proclaim and promote over man-made organizations and comes against self-exaltation which costs God's potential sheep every penny they can get.

To exposes their divided bondage of sheep who don't know the true shepherd, from the one perpetrating the only one that can keep you, heal you, deliver you, and make you free to love beyond their doctrine and give you eternal life and access into His Kingdom. Don't bank on becoming one when you die and go to heaven especially after hearing this Truth about becoming one in JESUS. If you reject Him now, you might find yourself separated with the workers of iniquity boasting in all the good works you've done along with all the other groups who walk in the flesh, confessing King James not King JESUS. Look again at the root of it all. Men not living by every Word that proceeds out of the mouth of GOD.

Truly understand also, that scripture interpreted correctly helps us understand that the Father does nothing without His Word. So, let us not be deceived any longer and make sure, very sure, our definition of the Word of God is the only true and living, "infallible" Word that is God.

Using your preferred translation of scripture, check out what Paul wrote in 2 Corinthians 12:6-11.

Never taking into account we never pray to it or worship it, give it praise, obey it, Hear it, talk, or let it walk.

People will say and do what the Spirit they are led by dictates pretty much keeping them in a state of seeking the Truth or opposed to knowing Him. There's a difference in residing in that place of rest, where we're kept by the power of His Word rather than being dependent on someone to keep them encouraged from week to week.

Here is the relationship between our Father and His Word made flesh. (Read John 17:1-8 again). Remember there's power in knowing who JESUS is (read Luke 3:21, 22 using your preferred translations of scripture).

Also to side with what the majority says, they never thought for a moment they must take responsibility for their own personal relationship with our Father and his Word which is Spirit and Truth opposed to other versions and different interpretations from the original inspired revelations. Every new versions purpose is to be a better version than the one another groups put out. Are all the religious groups' bibles worthy to be called anything other than another version?

Does the statement cover all the cult bibles and the Satanist bibles and the bibles named after men even like Hitler?

If the bible is the Word of God, is it God? If not, how do you explain the fact that God and His Word are one? Who speaks?

Can you explain that and keep from sounding too ridiculous? And keep a straight face in the process?

When people don't know the true Word of God and try and make something else that is not, God, but as good as God's Word, could it be that they idolize the thing they claim to be equal to God?

What is the danger of making something God or equal to God? Where do people get the power to separate God from His Word and make their version the Word of God? Because almost everyone is saying it doesn't make it right.

The bible, whichever one a person claims to be the Word of God; do they worship "it"; praise "it"; pray to "it"; does "it" speak to them or do they hear from any number of religious fallen Spirits? Outside, the Spirit of Unity found only in God, his Word, his Kingdom, his Truth. Etc.

Do you agree JESUS is the living Word of God? If your answer is yes then let's go on. If not, re-read what you've read.

The Word of God through JESUS said: John 15:7-8: "If you abide in me and my words abide in you ..." Can you hear what I hear? Then continue in his Word in unity with all that is subject to His Word. Who stands alone? And few are empowered to stand alone without Him.

Every problem and sickness JESUS, the Word made flesh, spoke to or touched, the problem changed and people were healed because of their faith in Him. Today is no different. No one can name a problem or sickness JESUS can't heal. Even a touch from Him before you hear His voice tells you everything is going to be alright. HE can speak to us any way HE chooses. All we have to do is believe. But to misunderstand His touch without His Word, people have been known to go their own way. When His touch was to draw them, not send them.

Look now at the Father's love for us. In that HE sent His Word and His Word healed us who believe. The relationship between Him and His Word is in perfect union. JESUS always said "the Words that I speak unto you are not just a man's, but those of My Father." HE would say things like "the Words that I speak unto you they are Spirit and they are Life." We, too, must say what HE says.

His commandments are good, even today. For the Word of King JESUS told us to follow peace with all men -- to "seek ye first the Kingdom of God and His righteousness" (read Matthew 6:33 using your preferred translation of scripture). Have we obeyed Him?

I pray his Word has found a place in your Heart. His Word is not confined to just 66 books but the Spirit of the Word is still just as powerful and sweet as HE was when they were first spoken. (Read John 21:25 and Matthew 5:1-12 using your preferred translations of scripture). Matthew quoted JESUS, the Word of God and God cannot lie. Now, catch the Spirit of Him that liveth and claim your blessing. Isn't HE good? Stay with Him. Being mindful that HE said HE would never leave you or forsake you.

Prayer will not be a one-way conversation but we who are converted and understand the Kingdom of God is within us will learn to live, really live, by every Word that proceeds out of our Father.

JESUS would say things like: "my doctrine is not mine but Him that sent me. Read John 7:16-18 using your preferred translations of scripture and continue to read while seeking Him Who answers from the position of the Creator of the universe.
"The Words that I speak unto you, I speak not of myself (John 14:8-10). May the Spirit give you ears to hear and to listen to the Father talk about his Son, JESUS, as in Mark 1:9-13 "and it came to pass . . ." Don't confuse the Spirit of Truth and Unity.

As you become transformed by the Word of God, your understanding will be transformed to another dimension and to realize your life is not your own and the more you give up, the more you will find your place in Him. For what could be better than to live in His love, His joy and

His peace in the Holy Ghost completely satisfied in that place of rest?

After humbling ourselves like a little child whose trust is in someone else, faith in God's Word which is Spirit and Truth, must be received into our Spirits empowering us to govern the flesh and see beyond the natural. Followers of Him through obedience to what we hear above the earthly words man uses to impress people and sell products. Words from the Father, the Son or the Holy Spirit.

If anyone doesn't know Who the Word of God is then how can they be as effective in the work of the Kingdom? For we are to be Sons of the Most High, Ambassadors of the invisible Kingdom, echoing the Words of the King into the natural realm where one Word from God could change their life forever, even a whole generation.

I may not be the most intelligent person of my generation, but the simplicity of the gospel is this: nothing qualifies us like simple obedience to the Truth.

Most people are obedient to a lot of different things, even religious things influenced by fallen religious Spirits once submitted to the Truth.

Amazingly, it is possible to be able to hear the Word of God and not do what is heard.

Because his Words have the creative power to give life, his Word also speaks blessings and the power to make alive things said thousands of years ago echoed from eternity into time even to this generation. His Word always leads back to Him, not men who can't keep themselves?

If you make your bible (or any one of hundreds of bibles) the only infallible Word of God, the Spirit of deception will give you, along with that lie, the fruit of his hidden motive -- division from the Truth Himself, clearly seen in division.

My prayer is that someday we all will understand the Word of our Father. The Son is the Word and we must hear what the Spirit is saying to His Church. God and his Word are One and in order for us to be one with Him, we too must be knowledgeable of Who the Word of God is. For how many people do you know who don't understand the relationship between the Father and the Son and how the Spirit of His Word can manifest in and through whoever has an ear to hear?

Look at the Word of God, Who cannot lie, for HE explained over and over and over again throughout His ministry, exactly what was settled in heaven before the world began regarding Him as the perfect Lamb of God. And, that HE would indeed suffer at the hands of men and be crucified but had the power to take His life up again. So, even the garden experience was settled before HE got to the garden as agonizing as that experience was. The Word of God could not return to the Father without accomplishing that which HE had sent it to do. That's another reason, in order to be like JESUS, we too must have the Word of God ruling within us. For we are to be a living sacrifice, holy and acceptable unto our God and Father. If Christ be in you, HE will take you through anything you have to experience. If you put your trust in Him Whom you know, HE can take you through the valley of the shadow of death because HE got the victory over death, hell and the grave. Above just reading about Him, experience His Word directly to you being unique in your own special way. There is a Word just for you to establish you, keep you, give you purpose and give you an inheritance in the Kingdom of God with JESUS and all the heavenly host. Having the power to become Sons like Him even priests and kings unto our God.

You must not go into this book with a misunderstanding of the true and living almighty Word of God. You may very well use scripture (as you understand it), to even oppose the true Word of God Himself especially when you are so sure one of the other versions they believe is the only infallible Word of God.

Looking back at scripture we can clearly see how those in some kind of leadership role, really have misused scripture. In trying to keep the letter without the Spirit of the One Who was sent to lead the way, they would look for an opportunity to stone someone to death just out of tradition. Preachers today have their own way of killing people with the letter, and call it stepping on toes. The problem with most is that they themselves cannot stand correction. Is not this the reason most cell groups get started in the first place? Oh, I know they say God is made up of 66 books of the testimonies of dead souls whose recording was of Him but, most if not all, had a personal relationship with Him. In true fellowship with Him, we can have fellowship with each other if we can agree. But, our definition in English, or whatever language, must agree with those of our Father. One more example of the sacrifice HE made as our perfect offering to redeem us back to our Father.

HE suffered long with even his followers' unbelief. We read in the Book of Philippians, the 2nd Chapter, verses 5-11 how we should "let this mind be in you, which was also in Christ JESUS, His being in the form of God, thought it not robbery to be equal with God . . . . . And that every tongue should confess that JESUS Christ is LORD, to the glory of God the Father." Do we truly understand how we too can be included in glorifying his name?

GLORIFY YOUR NAME IN US

For years, that was the sum total of my Song unto my Father.
An offering in Song acknowledging Who could bless us like He can.

What would bring more glory to our Father than for Him to see His children open to Him to love one another through us? As we die to self so HE can live in us, we will see Him love others past our petty differences like baptism if we were baptized in His love, joy and peace. If we were baptized in His righteousness, mercy and grace, we would be baptized in His name, His Spirit and in His Word.

Did you know that when we die to self HE resurrects us unto a new life in Him? No more our own, we've been bought with a price. If we are going to be One in Him we must allow the JESUS in us to manifest Himself through us. HE did not promote another Kingdom, another Spirit, another pastor or another word other than the Father's Word, His purpose and His will. Are we to follow JESUS, or Paul? You are not to camp out in the epistles and not unite in what JESUS said!

As we obey the command to love, let's do as one writer quotes the very Words of God: Isaiah 1:18,19: "Come now, and let us reason together," Says the LORD, "Though your sins are like scarlet, They shall be as white as snow; Though they are red like crimson, They shall be as wool."

You will know beyond a shadow of a doubt the answer to that age-old question: how can we be one? How? Trust and obey the Word HE speaks to you which is the Spirit of Truth.

Satan only deceived Adam's bride about one thing: what God said not to do. There are thousands of things the last Adam's bride has been deceived about "which JESUS will deliver us from". Let's look at just two:
    1. The first and most important is Who the Word of God is. Understanding Who HE is and on what everything else you will ever learn is hinged on. JESUS said to the unbelievers who did not receive His Word – John 5:39-40 "search the scriptures for in them you think ye have eternal life: and they are they which testify of Me." "And ye will not come to Me, that ye might have life."

    2. Second is baptism. The Spirit of Unity says, what's wrong with being baptized in the Name of the Father, the Son, and the Holy Ghost?

If you haven't skipped over the earlier chapters and have heard from the Spirit of Truth, you know Who JESUS is. And there is One, Who the name was given to, Who is one with the Father and the Holy Ghost. HE is none other than the Living Eternal Life-giving, Creative, and Almighty Word of God. To be baptized in the Holy Ghost is to be baptized in JESUS: I'll give you some scriptures but don't forget the little exercise we did throughout this book. Never exalt anything in the natural over the work of the Spirit.

In Acts 1:2-5; [2] until the day in which He was taken up, after He through the Holy Spirit had given commandments to the apostles whom He had chosen, [3] to whom He also presented Himself alive after His suffering by many infallible proofs, being seen by them during forty days and speaking of the things pertaining to the kingdom of God. [4] And being assembled together with *them,* He commanded them not to depart from Jerusalem, but to wait for the Promise of the Father, "which," *He said,* "you have heard from Me; [5] for John truly baptized with water, but you shall be baptized with the Holy Spirit not many days from now."

Acts 1:8 [8] But you shall receive power when the Holy Spirit has come upon you; and you shall be witnesses to Me in Jerusalem, and in all Judea and Samaria, and to the end of the earth."

John 20:21-23 [21] So Jesus said to them again, "Peace to you! As the Father has sent Me, I also send you." [22] And when He had said this, He breathed on *them,* and said to them, "Receive the Holy Spirit. [23] If you forgive the sins of any, they are forgiven them; if you retain the *sins* of any, they are retained."

Matthew 28:10: [10] Then Jesus said to them, "Do not be afraid. Go *and* tell My brethren to go to Galilee, and there they will see Me."

Matthew 28:16-20: [16] Then the eleven disciples went away into Galilee, to the mountain which Jesus had appointed for them. [17] When they saw Him, they worshiped Him; but some doubted. [18] And Jesus came and spoke to them, saying, "All authority has been given to Me in heaven and on earth. [19] Go therefore and make disciples of all the nations, baptizing them in the name of the Father and of the Son and of the Holy Spirit, [20] teaching them to observe all things that I have commanded you; and lo, I am with you always, *even* to the end of the age." Amen.

If any would still argue baptism by water, whatever way they do it, and uphold division over it, they're automatically in error in not keeping the unity of the faith. God knows how to correct his little ones through any of the gifts HE's given, especially if they will Hear and hold to the doctrine of the apostles and prophets (those that are true). It is a Spirit of division or misunderstanding for people to start a whole movement on baptism – water baptism at that. How long will we who can Hear stand apart and not together?

To show you my motives are pure, I'm not promoting anything other than our Father whose name will be glorified. His Kingdom and the Church HE's building putting us together as the Body of Christ, one with Him in total submission to His Will, led by the Word of God.

Everyone who confesses to be the church and doesn't know His Voice is none of His. Then, whose sheep are they? You must read between the lines.

Our Will or His Will

Some of you have been given the gifts of apostles, prophets, or evangelists but could never rise above the pastor who thinks those gifts must remain under their authority. Well, for the sake of whatever gift or office you are called to, the gift that lights your fire when you hear it is because you can relate to what you've been called to be. There are prophets determined to be "the" pastor and neglecting what they were called to do. Or, on the other hand, when you have a pastor trying to be an apostle or prophet and it's sort of like the milkman doing your heart transplant without being truly qualified.

"Father, how can I explain to my brothers and sisters your love for them is extended to us all by correcting us?" I could say teaches us, but it's easier to reject teachings then stern correction. But His Word loves us even when HE corrects us.

Have you ever tried talking to someone who was hard of hearing or deaf? Or, if God doesn't open their ears to hear. Well, bear with me as I repeat myself in my writings. Some people will read this book with the same mentality as they would in reading the daily news. But, if I consistently repeat myself in drilling the point home, that the Word of God was made flesh and blood, not pen and paper, the workers of iniquity will see this as a direct assault on their livelihood, on their building project, or their hopes of having a big church (building to corral lost sheep). Church/religion is big, big business - a career choice. For,have you noticed that most religious leaders are experts at giving out correction week after week, but now that correction is at their door, let's see how they receive correction or go on as if the Spirit is talking to everyone but them?

If you're seated with JESUS in heavenly places, sit back and watch the easily offended react in offense at the Spirit and my writings. His Truth is searching their hearts continuously; his judgments are all true. There are many ways the workers of iniquity will respond or even keep quiet or go away. The reason some leaders don't want to be corrected is: they're really playing out the role of "the" pastor. What they don't know is that lying Spirits have their rewards. They're closed to the Word of God through correction, by man or the Spirit.

The bible shows us we are to die daily to self and crucify the flesh, to stop being self-centered, self-willed, and self-seeking. At some point and time, we too must have a Gethsemane experience in earnest prayer where we, too, like JESUS, make that decision. Our Father's will is better for us and the reward far outweighs the pain we must endure which gets easier to bear day by day all for serving others who don't know the almighty, all powerful Word of God, Who is God. Victory in the suffering of this present world will be for a stand of righteousness for and from them that oppose themselves. No more I, but Christ that liveth in me. Living and dying in submission to the Word of God, in you.

I'm becoming more and more acutely aware within myself that the more I die, the more HE lives. And in this body, I'm witnessing for myself Christ working in me, speaking through us who believe, experiencing what the early church experienced, who lived and loved everything the Word revealed to them. In so much as all they wanted to do was stay before Him eventually recording, in writing, the wonderful Words they heard, for the good of all men who would believe.

God's Word is still speaking today to this generation, just like theirs. But, for most people, their only knowledge of God's Word is what they read, written in another generation years before the living Word of God through JESUS said. "My sheep will know My Voice and another they will not follow". And explained that HE was the fulfillment of all Truth written when some couldn't receive Him over their knowledge and limited understanding.

The Word of God said, recorded in John 6:37-40 (read: using your preferred translation of scripture) and John 6:45 says: "it is written . . . Cometh unto me." And Mark 4:35 reads "for Whosoever shall do the will of God, the same is my brother, and sister, and mother." If you confess to say only what your bible says, check again whose copyright version you believe is speaking to you then, ask yourself, where is their bible version found in scripture and what Spirit is speaking? Or do all bibles say what people interpret them to say? Or could it be those other voices JESUS spoke about?

Every voice we hear is not the Word of God and not in unity from his Kingdom. Why do all wrong interpretations end up in division? Can you believe JESUS prayed for us to be one with one LORD, one faith, one baptism, one, one, one in Him?

JESUS, in teaching his disciples to pray, said "pray: our Father which art in heaven (read: Matthew 6:9, 10 using your preferred translation of scripture). If at this point you don't know the difference in God's Word, Who is Spirit and Truth and even though man is writing about things JESUS said and did with pen and paper, you're still not free to really walk by faith if your faith is solely based on what you can see.

Think for a moment, about the will of our Father here on earth. Even today, in 2015, looking back to the very beginning, Adam gave up dominion. But the Word restored the Kingdom back to man. Being governed again by the Word of the king, we will be able to make the Kingdoms of this world the Kingdoms of our God, and reverse or flip the script of the enemy.

You must understand that Lucifer and a host of angels were cast out of heaven where everything was righteous, pure and true. Everything was submitted to the will and Word of God. All the magnificent wonders of heaven were viewed and enjoyed by everything in the Kingdom of Heaven, things never seen by man and things yet, to be seen. We're talking about the Kingdom of the only true God of all creation. Some things in His Kingdom are unspeakable. When man disobeyed the Word of God, HE lost his position of ruling as kings here on earth with dominion given by the King of Kings. Now, satan and all the angels that fell with Him, who only knew the wonderful things in heaven, know nothing but perversion in everything they did. All they had ever known in heaven was now demonstrated by unrighteous religious demons, lying devils, deceiving spirits. Even with a perverse experience of heaven, everything in heaven they knew is now void of grace and truth and no longer available to them by His Spirit. Fallen man without being led by the Truth, will be influenced by their fallen religious spirits, some obviously more religious than others.

What if we start marching to the will of God and Word of God and turn the perversion around, back to God for His glory? If only those who hear and know His Voice would obey the voice of the good shepherd. Or, do the voices of lying spirits that oppose the Truth have the ear of those who don't know the Truth? Take a good look at the Kingdoms of the world, and then look at how they can be turned around for good. Could it be that people who hear the good shepherd don't have the understanding that their gift is to be used to now come together as one?

I hate to offend you so early in this book but if you want to know the Truth, we will only be able to do His Will, when we're able to hear, know and obey His Word. No substitutions with our earthly writings and understanding for the Risen, Living Word of Almighty God, our Father. The work of spirits outside the Truth is confusion. I have only two questions again: 1) can we know His Voice, and do His Will? Or 2) will we ever agree in the scriptures apart from hearing Him?

The scriptures will look a lot different when we make them line up with the true author. Not every divided group insisting on making Him line up with their misinterpretations.

Giving up our will for His to be done is one of the greatest things we could ever do because today it seems as though everyone is doing his own thing and everyone has turned unto his own way but the Word of God even has an answer for that.

Know this: His Will is a Living Will filled with everything you will ever need in this life and forever. In His Will for you there is wisdom and the power to get wealth and the best explanation of wealth I've ever heard is: assets that produce income when you're not working. That my friend is the kind of wealth you can pass on to your children and your children's children. In the will are the keys given for access in and out of the Kingdom. An Eternal Kingdom from which you can draw as much peace as you need; as much power, and there's more out there.

Enough for everyone who will simply receive joy unspeakable. All the rewards of obeying the command to love are enough to share with everyone you meet, even your enemies, with the knowledge that God would fight your battles for you. This Living Will gives favor to your family and those who receive you.

People can talk their way out of just about anything even in rejecting the Truth, having never given up their free will as an offering unto God. A living sacrifice outweighs all our good works. Wars are started by men. People will sell others out for sex. By exercising their power they can take everything they can get from you and not give it a second thought.

Here's a word of wisdom to the wise. If you say JESUS lives in you, remember who the name JESUS was given to. The only reason you don't know His Voice is because the enemy's voices and all the distractions out lasted your patience to wait on an answer or a Word from God. Remember reading, "In your patience possess you your souls?" Wait on the LORD, again I say wait on the LORD.

I could spend a Whole chapter explaining His Will. Even the wealth of the unjust belongs to our Father. Untold treasures are in the living will of the only King over all the universe. Who in their right mind, who truly understands, would not give up their will for His? Here's a good place to give unto Him a pure free will offering.

Remember what we covered in Chapter 1 regarding the power in the Word of God. The Spirit and the power in what HE said back then to Solomon is alive today if we believe and obey what the Spirit is telling us to do today.

Because the deceiver deceived Adam it led to the whole human race falling from grace into sin. The only way back to a right relationship with our Father, Creator and Living God was for Him to redeem us back. HE had to reach us and HE did just that. HE got the attention of men by communicating to lost man by His Word, which is Spirit. At the appointed time, HE came to earth in the flesh and was able to make plain and fulfill all that the early writers wrote about Him after receiving revelation from God.

Think about this. The True Almighty Word of God, Who created all things said, "Let there be light". HE did not have to repeat Himself to make light continue to shine. Only man with a free will could disobey what God said.

But HE didn't leave us eternally separated from our life source because HE sent his Word into the natural realm to redeem us back to Himself. HE sent his own life giving Word in the form of a man. Gave his Word made flesh a name.

Speaking of the Word of God, Who is one with His Spirit? And one with His Creative Power to speak things into existence? Listen to the Spirit as to what JESUS, the Word of God, Who cannot lie said recorded in our earthly writing by eyewitnesses, such as John, right before HE left this earth to return to the Father. Like the centurion who believed JESUS could speak the Word only and his servant would be healed, believed for us to be one by faith in the Word of God Who lives. John 17:12-26, "while I was with them in the world, I kept them in Your name: those that thou gavest Me I have kept, and none of them is lost but the Son of perdition that the scripture might be fulfilled".

Now that you know Who spoke these Words over two thousand years ago, we can better comprehend the power to accomplish everything HE said. If there's a misprint or misinterpretation of translation, we still must rely on revelation from the Spirit to those whose motives are pure, whose hearts are toward the things of the Spirit where the power to accomplish His Will comes from, not double minded or easily offended, Self-centered, or self-exalting through earthly knowledge.

The job of mature Sons of the king is to echo the Words of the king into this realm from the Kingdom of Love, Joy and Peace in the Holy Ghost which is within us. Wherever and in whomever His Word rules, there His Kingdom is established.

As priest and kings united with JESUS (Whom you know), we're to stand with Him in the gap for the people. The Father has called and, as kings, we must declare the declarations of the King of Kings.

An aid to help us get to where HE has purposed for us to be is one more thing we need that's very, very important. Believe when working with each other in love, mercy, righteousness and forgiveness towards one another. Knowing all division comes from the deceiver, the Spirit of misunderstanding, even the father of all lies.

We need patience in waiting on God to answer prayers. If or when our faith gets weak, we can live forever off the last Word spoken to us, for his Word is eternal meat by which we live. To you who know and believe, simply ask anything in line with His Will in faith, and it will be given unto you. But, we can't put Him in a box as to the time of the manifestation of what's being requested.

In most cases, there are things in us that need to be worked out. For HE sees everything involved in blessing us and adding no sorrow. Behind the scenes are obstacles, traps, family, and friends and even self-people who hate you and will oppose even your prayers and good will towards them.

But to sum up, again in plain old English the best way to know and follow JESUS is by knowing Him by His Word. For the living Word speaks in many ways you must be open to listen. Some people have been led without being knowledgeable of who was doing the leading. Their senses were tuned into other Spirits. But for you, in this day and age we can and will be much more effective when we know Him and HE knows us. So we can better teach our children and our children's children so they don't spend as much time building their own little kingdoms and drawing people to a man-made organization. I don't want to get ahead of myself by explaining further because in the chapters following this one, HE will further explain His Will and the answer to all our problems.

No one knowingly prays to, worships and calls their bible, God. But, to call it the Word of God is the same thing, for God and his Word cannot be separated.

Finally:

PLEASE ALLOW THE WORD OF GOD TO BE THE FINAL EDITOR

Timeline of Bible Translation History

1,400 BC: The first written Word of God: The Ten Commandments delivered to Moses.

500 BC: Completion of All Original Hebrew Manuscripts which make up The 39 Books of the Old Testament.

200 BC: Completion of the Septuagint Greek Manuscripts which contain The 39 Old Testament Books AND 14 Apocrypha Books.

1st Century AD: Completion of All Original Greek Manuscripts which make up The 27 Books of the New Testament.

315 AD: Athenasius, the Bishop of Alexandria, identifies the 27 books of the New Testament which are today recognized as the canon of scripture.

382 AD: Jerome's Latin Vulgate Manuscripts Produced which contain All 80 Books (39 Old Test. + 14 Apocrypha + 27 New Test).

500 AD: Scriptures have been Translated into Over 500 Languages.

600 AD: LATIN was the Only Language Allowed for Scripture.

995 AD: Anglo-Saxon (Early Roots of English Language) Translations of The New Testament Produced.

1384 AD: Wycliffe is the First Person to Produce a (Hand-Written) manuscript Copy of the Complete Bible; All 80 Books.

1455 AD: Gutenberg Invents the Printing Press; Books May Now be mass-Produced Instead of Individually Hand-Written. The First Book Ever Printed is Gutenberg's Bible in Latin.

1516 AD: Erasmus Produces a Greek/Latin Parallel New Testament.

1522 AD: Martin Luther's German New Testament.

1526 AD: William Tyndale's New Testament; The First New Testament printed in the English Language.

1535 AD: Myles Coverdale's Bible; The First Complete Bible printed in the English Language (80 Books: O.T. & N.T. & Apocrypha).

1537 AD: Tyndale-Matthews Bible; The Second Complete Bible printed in English. Done by John "Thomas Matthew" Rogers (80 Books).

1539 AD: The "Great Bible" Printed; The First English Language Bible Authorized for Public Use (80 Books).

1560 AD: The Geneva Bible Printed; The First English Language Bible to add Numbered Verses to Each Chapter (80 Books).

1568 AD: The Bishops Bible Printed; The Bible of which the King James was a Revision (80 Books).

1609 AD: The Douay Old Testament is added to the Rheims New Testament (of 1582) Making the First Complete English Catholic Bible; Translated from the Latin Vulgate (80 Books).

1611 AD: The King James Bible Printed; Originally with All 80 Books. The Apocrypha was Officially Removed in 1885 Leaving Only 66 Books.

1782 AD: Robert Aitken's Bible; The First English Language Bible (KJV) Printed in America.

1791 AD: Isaac Collins and Isaiah Thomas Respectively Produce the First Family Bible and First Illustrated Bible Printed in America. Both were King James Versions, with All 80 Books.

1808 AD: Jane Aitken's Bible (Daughter of Robert Aitken); The First Bible to be Printed by a Woman.

1833 AD: Noah Webster's Bible; After Producing his Famous Dictionary, Webster Printed his Own Revision of the King James Bible.

1841 AD: English Hexapla New Testament; an Early Textual Comparison showing the Greek and 6 Famous English Translations in Parallel Columns.

1846 AD: The Illuminated Bible; The Most Lavishly Illustrated Bible printed in America. A King James Version, with All 80 Books.

1863 AD: Robert Young's "Literal" Translation; often criticized for being so literal that it sometimes obscures the contextual English meaning.

1885 AD: The "English Revised Version" Bible; The First Major English Revision of the KJV.

1901 AD: The "American Standard Version"; The First Major American Revision of the KJV.

1952 AD: The "Revised Standard Version" (RSV); said to be a Revision of the 1901 American Standard Version, though more highly criticized.

1971 AD: The "New American Standard Bible" (NASB) is Published as a "Modern and Accurate Word for Word English Translation" of the Bible.

1973 AD: The "New International Version" (NIV) is Published as a "Modern and Accurate Phrase for Phrase English Translation" of the Bible.

1982 AD: The "New King James Version" (NKJV) is Published as a "Modern English Version Maintaining the Original Style of the King James."

1990 AD: The "New Revised Standard Version" (NRSV); further revision of 1952 RSV, (itself a revision of 1901 ASV), criticized for "gender inclusiveness".

2002 AD: The English Standard Version (ESV) is Published as a translation to bridge the gap between the accuracy of the NASB and the readability of the NIV.

40172471R00083

Made in the USA
Middletown, DE
05 February 2017